RICH METHOD 2.0

First edition. July 4, 2025.

ISBN: 979-8231092338

AF785071

Written by David Sandua.

RICH Method 2.0

Personal Finance and Economic Freedom After the Crisis

DAVID SANDUA

Rich Method 2.0

Electronic and Paperback Edition.

"The most powerful asset a person can own is their own financial education."
***Robert Kiyosaki**, author of Rich Dad, Poor Dad*

INDEX

I. INTRODUCTION

Amidst the din of everyday life, many individuals feel the sting of financial uncertainty, navigating a precarious balance between survival and aspiration. The aftermath of the recent economic crisis has amplified these feelings, compelling many to reassess their financial habits and priorities. In this exploration of personal finance through the lens of the RICH Method 2.0, it becomes crucial to acknowledge the pervasive mistakes made during previous downturns. Overreliance on credit, poor budgeting skills, and a lack of financial knowledge were widespread issues that left many unprepared and vulnerable. By examining these challenges through both hard statistics and personal anecdotes, we can better understand the urgency for a structured approach to achieving economic freedom. The juxtaposition of the abstract numbers with visceral stories of families struggling to maintain dignity and stability will set the stage for a comprehensive analysis of reshaping ones financial landscape.

Transitioning from the economic fallout, the RICH Method 2.0 emerges as a beacon of pragmatic guidance, comprising five essential steps to foster financial resilience. Each component—Reinvesting wisely, Improving expense efficiency, Creating a solid safety net, and Harnessing purpose-driven saving—serves as a foundation upon which individuals can build their financial well-being. The integration of contemporary data regarding savings rates and mortgage debt levels will illustrate the dire need for these principles, emphasizing that economic recovery requires more than passive hope; it necessitates actionable knowledge. Engaging personal stories of individuals who took the leap into financial literacy will complement this data, showcasing transformative journeys that defy the doom-laden narrative surrounding financial crises. This merger of experiences with benchmarks for success will offer not just reassurance, but a framework for sustainable change.

As we delve deeper into the methodology, it becomes important to offer pragmatic exercises and reflective opportunities that empower readers to take ownership of their financial destiny. Each chapter will conclude with straightforward tasks—spreadsheets designed to track spending or prompts that challenge ingrained habits—inviting readers to internalize the new principles presented. This hands-on approach not only reinforces learning but also catalyzes actionable behavior change, fostering a sense of control over one's finances. In an age where financial literacy can feel out of reach, the RICH Method 2.0 promises accessible, disciplined, and effective steps toward achieving economic freedom. Thus, by framing this journey through compelling narratives and clear directives, readers will find themselves equipped not only to survive future economic crises but to thrive in a landscape of opportunity and growth.

OVERVIEW OF THE FINANCIAL CRISIS

As the economy expanded in the early 2000s, many families found themselves caught in the allure of easy credit and escalating home values. This seductive environment fostered a sense of financial security, prompting numerous individuals to take on substantial mortgage debts without understanding the underlying risks. When the housing bubble burst, these same families faced foreclosure, leaving many questioning their financial literacy and preparedness. Anecdotes from families who watched their dreams of homeownership unravel serve as poignant reminders of the human cost of financial missteps. In retrospect, a lack of comprehensive financial education facilitated reckless borrowing behaviors, which only intensified the crisis. For those aspiring for economic freedom, recognizing these patterns of excess can serve as a foundation for reshaping their financial strategies. The first step is confronting these lessons the previous generation overlooked, ensuring that they do not repeat the same costly errors.

Not only did the crisis expose vulnerabilities in personal finance practices, but it also revealed systemic weaknesses within banking institutions and regulations. During this turbulent period, hard data painted a grim picture, showing skyrocketing unemployment rates and a plummeting economy. Interviews with economists and financial advisors from that time highlight a consensus on the urgent need for reform in lending practices and increased oversight of financial institutions. For many, the crisis was a wake-up call, one that underscored the importance of a diversified financial portfolio and prudent risk management. It became evident that building an economic safety net, much like households in previous generations had done, was now more essential than ever. Understanding these macroeconomic factors lays the groundwork for individuals seeking to not only recover from past mistakes but also build a financially resilient future. Redeeming the lessons of the financial crisis becomes even more impactful when combined with personal storytelling. Consider the experience of a single mother who, after losing her job during the recession, turned to savings and budgeting to navigate her financial turmoil. Her journey towards stability involved evaluating her expenses and embracing a frugal lifestyle, harnessing purpose-driven saving strategies to allocate funds effectively. Such narratives illustrate the tangible evolution from devastation to financial empowerment, echoing the principles of the "RICH Method 2.0." By implementing structured practices such as reallocating resources and establishing a solid safety net, individuals can move from a crisis mentality to one focused on sustainable growth. Practical exercises involving goal-setting and budget tracking empower others to adopt similar resilience strategies, inviting readers to take active steps towards financial control amidst broader economic uncertainties.

IMPORTANCE OF PERSONAL FINANCE

Navigating the financial landscape after a crisis requires a profound understanding of personal finance, where individual choices shape broader economic outcomes. Picture a young couple, Sarah and Tom, who, after facing layoffs during the recent downturn, realized the fragility of their financial situation. They hadn't prioritized budgeting before, and the once-comfortable lifestyle crumbled quickly under unexpected expenses. As they reconstructed their approach, they discovered the transformative power of personal finance education. It became clear that cultivating a proactive mindset around money management was essential, not just for surviving but for thriving in an uncertain economy. This scenario echoes the common experiences of many families, illustrating that the first step towards economic freedom lies in recognizing the importance of financial literacy. By providing accessible knowledge and fostering essential skills, individuals can significantly alter their financial trajectories and create stability, laying a foundation for future wealth accumulation. Incorporating systematic financial habits is crucial for resilience against economic shocks. Consider the case of Maria, a single mother who initially struggled with impulse spending and debt accumulation. After participating in a community financial workshop, she learned about the RICH Method 2.0, which emphasized the importance of improving expense efficiency. By tracking her expenditure and identifying unnecessary costs, Maria transformed her financial habits, enabling her to funnel money into savings for her children's education. This story highlights a fundamental truth: small, disciplined adjustments in everyday financial decisions can lead to substantial improvements over time. Such practical examples reinforce the idea that personal finance is not solely about theoretical knowledge; it's about developing actionable plans that promote sound financial health. Emphasizing this transformative process serves as a motivational call for individuals to initiate their journeys toward economic autonomy, demonstrating that the power to reshape one's financial future lies within reach.

Personal finance serves as a vital component of long-term economic freedom, particularly when harnessed through purpose-driven saving. The journeys of individuals like Jake, who turned his side hustle into a thriving business after reevaluating his savings goals, illustrate the potential for financial empowerment. He adopted the principles of the RICH Method 2.0, focusing on reinvesting wisely and establishing a solid safety net before expanding his ventures. This approach not only safeguarded Jake against unpredictable market conditions but also underscored the necessity of having a clear financial vision. In essence, purpose-driven saving connects personal aspirations with practical financial strategies, enabling individuals to pursue growth while safeguarding their interests. As the landscape of personal finance continues to evolve, the urgency of adopting these principles in daily practice cannot be overstated. The call to action is clear: readers must take deliberate steps to redefine their financial futures, laying the groundwork for a more secure and prosperous life.

INTRODUCTION TO THE RICH METHOD 2.0

In the wake of the last recession, countless individuals found themselves navigating an economic landscape that seemed foreign and unsettling. Many grappled with the repercussions of poor financial decisions, often rooted in a lack of education and awareness about personal finance. The RICH Method 2.0 emerges as a timely and structured response to these challenges, emphasizing a proactive approach to financial management. By diagnosing common pitfalls, such as excessive reliance on credit and underestimating savings, this method equips individuals with tangible strategies to take control of their finances. It encourages a systemic evaluation of one's financial habits through relatable narratives of families who not only faced but overcame these obstacles, illustrating the methods practicality and relevance in today's economy.

The core of the RICH Method 2.0 is a five-step framework designed to guide individuals toward economic freedom. Each component—Reinvesting wisely, Improving expense efficiency, Creating a solid safety net, and Harnessing purpose-driven saving—provides an actionable pathway based on real-life experiences and contemporary data. Families who invested in education or side businesses witnessed substantial returns, revealing how reinvestment leads to wealth accumulation. The Improving expense efficiency step stands out, showcasing a family's success story where a few small tweaks in budgeting translated into significant savings. This method is not about overnight riches; rather, it fosters discipline and strategic thinking, proven essential in achieving financial stability. The stories of those who have applied the RICH Method underscore its effectiveness and relatability to anyone seeking improvement.

The introduction of the RICH Method 2.0 serves as an empowering invitation to rethink financial strategies amidst ongoing economic uncertainties. Each chapter concludes with practical exercises that reinforce the concepts introduced, encouraging readers to adopt these principles actively. Simple yet effective tools such as creating a budget spreadsheet or setting weekly savings challenges can facilitate gradual, meaningful changes in financial behavior. By emphasizing methodical steps rather than unrealistic promises, this approach demystifies financial growth and allows readers to visualize their progress. The journey toward economic freedom may be daunting, but the RICH Method 2.0 offers a clear roadmap, rooted in the understanding that sustained effort and informed decisions are the cornerstones of lasting financial well-being.

II. DIAGNOSIS OF THE FINANCIAL CRISIS

In an ever-evolving financial landscape, moments of profound crisis unveil the stark reality of individuals' financial illiteracy and misplaced confidence in economic systems. Many seasoned workers, believing themselves to be financially savvy, can recount harrowing tales of abrupt job loss or skyrocketing debt, driven by unsound mortgage practices. The financial crisis served as a harsh awakening for families across the globe, with data showing millions experiencing foreclosures and bankruptcies, often fueled by a lack of understanding of mortgage contracts and credit scores. Personal stories emerge—a single mother finding herself unable to pay her bills as her adjustable-rate mortgage spiraled out of control—underscoring the need for comprehensive financial education. Analyzing this landscape reveals a pressing need to identify and address the dangerous habits that proliferated prior to the crisis, ensuring that individuals can avoid making similar mistakes in the future and that financial freedom remains attainable. Delving further into the patterns of debt accumulation during the crisis, it becomes evident that a significant disconnect existed between consumer behavior and financial realities. Predatory lending practices, coupled with inflated asset prices, fostered an environment in which individuals were not only encouraged but felt compelled to overextend themselves financially. Through the lens of a family whose aspirations for home ownership transformed into financial despair, it becomes clear that the allure of easy credit often masks underlying risks. As families borrowed beyond their means, credit card debt soared, and personal savings plummeted—factors that led to a cascading effect of financial instability during the economic downturn. In the wake of these revelations, it is crucial to confront these damaging debt patterns, recalibrating approaches to personal finance with a focus on sustainable practices, thus paving the way for future economic empowerment. Amidst the turmoil of the financial crisis, a deeper examination reveals that the absence of a solid financial safety net significantly exacerbated individual hardships. Many individuals, caught off-guard by the sudden economic downturn, lacked the cushion of savings to weather the storm. Conversations with financial advisors reflect a consensus on the transformative power of establishing an emergency fund, even if it begins humbly. Real stories of individuals who prioritized saving—shifting their mindset from immediate gratification to future security—often reveal paths to resilience and recovery from financial distress. As we assess the lessons from the crisis, the call to action is clear: one must take deliberate steps to build a safety net that provides not only a shield from unforeseen circumstances but also fosters a mindset shift towards proactive financial management. By embracing this disciplined approach, individuals can reclaim control over their financial destinies, thus emerging resilient and ready to seize opportunities for economic freedom.

Indicator	Value
Real GDP Decline	4.2% contraction between Q4 2007 and Q2 2009
Unemployment Rate Peak	10.0% in October 2009
Total Job Losses	Approximately 8.7 million jobs lost from February 2008 to February 2010
Household Net Worth Decline	$11.5 trillion (17.3%) decrease from Q2 2007 to Q1 2009
Stock Market Decline	Dow Jones Industrial Average fell by 53% between October 2007 and March 2009
Home Equity Loss	Total home equity in the U.S. dropped from $13 trillion in 2006 to $8.8 trillion by mid-2008
Foreclosure Rate	Approximately 17% of homeowners were 'upside down' on their mortgages as of January 2015

Financial Crisis Impact on U.S. Economy and Households

COMMON MISTAKES MADE BY INDIVIDUALS

Amidst the backdrop of financial missteps, many individuals fall into the trap of neglecting a comprehensive understanding of their spending habits. A common scenario involves an emerging professional who impulsively buys the latest gadgets without considering their overall budget. This disconnect often leads to a cycle of debt, pushing them further into a financial quagmire. Recent data reveals that nearly 60% of millennials reportedly live paycheck to paycheck, largely due to unregulated spending behaviors, a trend amplified during economic downturns. These individuals frequently overlook the importance of tracking expenses on a granular level, which is pivotal for identifying unnecessary expenditures. This lack of fiscal insight not only hinders immediate financial stability but also disrupts long-term wealth accumulation. In light of this, practical exercises, such as maintaining a weekly expense log, become invaluable tools. By fostering discipline in monitoring expenditures, individuals can cultivate better financial awareness and ultimately steer clear of common pitfalls.

Transitioning from impulsive spending, another prevalent mistake is underestimating the impact of debt management. Picture a family that, buoyed by desperate promises of promotions and salary increases, takes on substantial loans to fund a lavish lifestyle. Unfortunately, when the expected raises do not materialize, the burden of debt becomes unmanageable. Current statistics suggest that unsecured debt continues to rise alarmingly, often spiraling out of control for individuals ill-equipped with the tools for effective debt reduction. This miscalculation not only places immediate financial stability at risk but also erects barriers to future opportunities and investments. Individuals need to embrace actionable strategies, like the debt avalanche or debt snowball methods, to tackle their loans effectively.

A practical exercise here could involve creating a prioritized debt repayment plan, empowering individuals to take charge of their financial futures and demystify the overwhelming nature of debt. The glaring mistake of neglecting an emergency fund serves as a stark reminder of the resilience required in personal finance. Imagine a young professional, eager to thrive yet wholly unprepared for unexpected setbacks like job loss or medical crises. The absence of a financial cushion can quickly escalate into a desperate situation. Data indicates that only about one in four Americans have enough savings to cover three months of living expenses, leaving many vulnerable in times of crisis. This gap reflects a broader issue of financial education where the foundational concept of savings is often overlooked. By adopting a proactive strategy, such as setting aside a small percentage of income each month, individuals can create stability amidst uncertainty. A suggested exercise could involve reviewing monthly financial inflows and outflows to allocate resources methodically toward building an emergency fund. This practice not only fosters financial security but also cultivates a mindset ready to confront life's unpredictability.

Mistake	Impact
Lack of Financial Literacy	Individuals with limited financial knowledge are more likely to make costly financial errors, such as under participating in financial markets, inadequately diversifying their portfolios, and choosing mortgage contracts poorly. These mistakes can lead to higher debt levels and financial instability.
Ignoring Credit Reports	Over 80% of individuals do not regularly check their credit reports, increasing the risk of identity theft and financial fraud. Regular monitoring is essential to detect and address unauthorized activities promptly.
Overreliance on Credit Cards	Approximately 46% of Americans carry credit card debt, often due to high-interest rates and overspending. This can lead to prolonged debt cycles and financial stress.
Not Saving Adequately	Many individuals fail to save sufficiently, leaving them vulnerable to financial emergencies and retirement insecurity. Establishing an emergency fund and consistent savings habits are crucial for financial stability.
Mismanaging Debt	Carrying high-interest debt, such as credit card balances, without a clear repayment plan can lead to financial strain and reduced credit scores. Prioritizing debt repayment and avoiding minimum payments can mitigate these effects.

Common Financial Mistakes and Their Impact on Individuals

DEBT PATTERNS OBSERVED POST-CRISIS

In the wake of the recent financial crisis, individuals found themselves grappling with the weight of unprecedented debt levels. Families who once enjoyed a comfortable standard of living were faced with the harrowing reality of mortgage defaults and rising credit card balances. This financial burden not only threatened their immediate stability but also tarnished their credit scores, hindering future borrowing ability. Anecdotes abound of people who learned the hard way about the risks of over-leveraging, as illustrated by Maria and Pedro, a couple from Madrid. With a sizeable mortgage and consumer debt, they felt the squeeze when interest rates climbed post-crisis. Their story serves as a warning: understanding the dynamics of debt is paramount. Just as they recalibrated their financial behaviors, individuals can reassess their relationship with debt, making informed decisions that prioritize long-term financial health.

Transitioning from the crisis has revealed distinct debt patterns that reflect broader economic and societal shifts. Recent data indicates a rise in student loan debt alongside a decline in traditional credit usage, as consumers become more cautious with their finances. Interviews with financial educators highlight a growing awareness among young adults regarding the necessity of budgeting and saving in an unpredictable economy. Javier, a recent college graduate, shares how he opted for public transportation rather than financing a car, allowing him to start his career with significantly less debt. Such stories illustrate a pivot away from reliance on credit cards towards prioritizing savings and responsible spending habits. It is evident that post-crisis, a profound shift in attitudes towards debt is taking root, encouraging individuals to develop a more disciplined and proactive approach to their financial futures.

To effectively navigate this new landscape, families must adopt an adaptable strategy that incorporates both data and personal experiences. The RICH Method 2.0 underscores the importance of creating a safety net and improving expense efficiency for debt management. Research reveals that households which allocate funds into emergency savings are better positioned to withstand unforeseen financial setbacks, effectively minimizing reliance on credit. This principle resonates with Anna, a single mother who embraced the tenets of the RICH Method after her own financial upheaval post-crisis. By diligently tracking her expenses and prioritizing savings, she transformed her financial trajectory, moving from anxiety-ridden debt to confident stability. As we reflect on these patterns, individuals are encouraged to integrate practical exercises into their financial routines, empowering them to build solid foundations for economic freedom while maintaining a committed focus on their long-term objectives.

Country	Debt-to-GDP Ratio Increase	Timeframe
Argentina	50%	3 Years
Indonesia	50%	3 Years
Brazil	25%	3 Years
Thailand	25%	3 Years
Turkey	25%	3 Years
Uruguay	25%	3 Years
Ecuador	0%	3 Years
Mexico	0%	3 Years
Russia	0%	3 Years

Post-Crisis Debt Patterns in Advanced Economies

GAPS IN FINANCIAL EDUCATION

Imagine a recent college graduate, brimming with ambition yet ill-prepared for the financial realities that lie ahead. While their academic training may have equipped them with critical thinking skills, it often overlooks practical financial education, leaving them vulnerable to common pitfalls such as credit card debt and inadequate savings. A startling statistic underscores this gap: studies reveal that only 17% of high school students received formal instruction in personal finance, which means a significant number of young adults step into the world without essential budgeting and investment know-how. The implications are dire; research shows that those lacking foundational financial literacy are not only more likely to fall into debt but also struggle to build wealth over time. This scenario highlights an urgent need for comprehensive financial education reform, aiming to bridge the disconnect between academic knowledge and real-world financial management.

The lack of financial education often comes at a steep price, as evidenced by stories of families torn apart by financial stress. A single parent, for instance, may find themselves drowning in loans while trying to provide for their children's future. Their journey illuminates the pervasive confusion surrounding financial options such as loans, savings accounts, and investment opportunities. A more informed population would make smarter choices, significantly altering the narrative. Interviews with financial advisors consistently reveal that tailored programs could address specific demographics, helping individuals navigate their unique financial circumstances. As such, advocating for inclusive financial curriculums could empower families to shift from survival mode to proactive wealth-building efforts. The question remains: how can society embrace the responsibility of fostering a financially literate populace, allowing personal finance education to become as fundamental as mathematics or science? To address these educational gaps, practical and engaging solutions are essential. Financial workshops or community classes can be introduced, drawing on easy to understand content and relatable anecdotes to capture participants interest. By providing hands-on experiences like budgeting exercises using real-life scenarios, these initiatives can demystify the complexities of personal finance. To put this concept into actionable terms, local governments and nonprofit organizations should collaborate to develop accessible resources, perhaps even partnering with successful entrepreneurs to inspire participants through their transformative stories. As individuals engage with finances from a young age, empowered by an understanding of the implications of their financial decisions, they will likely cultivate healthier relationships with money. The culmination of these efforts will not only address the immediate gaps in financial education but will also pave the way toward a future where economic freedom becomes attainable for all.

Percentage of students	
Lacking basic financial literacy	20%
With guaranteed access to a standalone Personal Finance course.	9.3%
With no access to financial education	5.6%
In schools with >75%. Black and Brown student population guarantee d access.	5%
In schools with <25%. Black and Brown student population guarantee d access.	14.3%
In schools with >75%. Free and Reduced Lunch eligibility guarantee d access.	5%
In schools with <25%. Free and Reduced Lunch eligibility guaranteed access.	12.5%
In rural locales guaranteed access.	14.3%
In suburban and town locales guaranteed access.	10%
In city locales guaranteed access.	5%

Financial Literacy and Education Gaps in the United States

III. THE IMPACT OF THE CRISIS ON PERSONAL FINANCE

In the wake of the crisis, millions found themselves grappling with the unavoidable reality of financial instability. Picture a family, once thriving in their well-balanced budget, suddenly forced to make difficult sacrifices after a job loss or drastic salary cut. Statistics reveal sobering truths—high unemployment rates surged alongside rising consumer debt, leaving many to rely on credit cards and loans just to maintain a semblance of normalcy. Such patterns not only led to immediate financial stress but also created long-term implications for personal credit ratings and borrowing capacity. For families navigating this tumultuous landscape, the need for financial education became more urgent than ever. As interviews with financial advisors show, understanding the roots of debt and cultivating proficient saving habits could empower individuals to reclaim control over their future.

Transitioning from crisis to opportunity mandated a mindset shift, compelling many to reevaluate their relationship with money. While financial despair often breeds an aversion to risks, countless success stories illustrate how this same crisis galvanized others to innovate and adapt. Entrepreneurs emerged from the rubble, creating new ventures by leveraging skills honed during the downturn. Their paths highlight a critical lesson embedded in the RICH Method 2.0: the importance of harnessing purpose-driven saving. This entails setting specific goals that resonate personally, transforming mundane saving practices into motivating endeavors. The recovery isn't just about survival; it's ultimately about fostering a proactive approach. As families learn from these narratives, they can envision their own financial futures not as a mere escape from hardship but as a vibrant opportunity for growth.

Navigating the nuances of economic recovery also calls for the establishment of a solid safety net, a lesson amplified by recent trials.

Many discovered that a lack of emergency funds could rear its head at the most inopportune moments, leaving them vulnerable to unforeseen expenses. Imagine a single parent with limited savings suddenly facing a medical emergency—options become precariously narrow. Amidst these challenges, the importance of efficient expense management rises to the forefront. Strategies encouraging smart budgeting became essential tools for families to fortify their financial stability. Simple weekly tracking of expenses encouraged accountability and sustainable habits. By systematically implementing small, attainable changes, individuals can gain confidence and clarity in their financial journeys. The call to action is clear: start today by assessing your current situation, setting a realistic budget, and committing to a savings challenge that aligns with your future aspirations.

CHANGES IN SAVINGS RATES

In the wake of economic uncertainty, many families experience profound shifts in their financial behaviors. Consider the Rodriguez family, who, after struggling to make ends meet during a recession, found themselves reevaluating their spending and saving practices. Data released from the Bank of Spain reveals that, during this crisis, the national savings rate dramatically increased as individuals prioritized financial security. This tendency highlights an essential lesson: when faced with financial instability, the instinct to save overindulging became apparent. Drawing from real-world experiences like that of the Rodriguez family, it becomes evident that adopting a savings-first mindset can lead to long-term financial resilience. As families adjusted their budgets, reducing discretionary spending, they illustrated a vital concept: necessity can indeed drive change, prompting them to concentrate on their savings to forge a safety net against future uncertainties.

The correlation between savings rates and economic recovery is hard to ignore. When savings increase, a dual-effect occurs: not only does individual financial security improve, but the overall economy gains liquidity, fueling growth. Look at the contrast between pre-crisis spending habits and the post-crisis shift towards savings. Many families, previously caught up in a cycle of consumerism, began making intentional choices, focusing on delaying gratification in favor of building a nest egg. To illustrate, a brief interview with a local financial advisor revealed that clients who were once reluctant to discuss saving now come in with plans for savings goals and emergency funds. This evolving mindset not only benefits individuals but also serves as a critical driver of economic recovery, enhancing overall consumer confidence and spending power. Understanding this shift is pivotal for anyone looking to navigate personal finance in the modern economy.

To harness the power of increased savings rates effectively, families must be intentional in translating their adjustments into sustainable financial habits. The transitioning narrative from reactive savings to proactive financial management is encapsulated by the "RICH Method 2.0." Families are encouraged not just to save, but to save with purpose—aligning their savings practices with their life goals and values. Those who prioritize long-term objectives such as education or retirement can create targeted savings plans that instill discipline and motivation. By implementing simple strategies, like setting up separate savings accounts for different goals, individuals can cultivate a clearer vision of their financial aspirations. As readers reflect on their own savings practices, they are invited to engage in a personal exercise: chart their monthly expenditures against their savings contributions, striving to enhance awareness and identify areas for improvement. This straightforward approach allows individuals to take tangible steps towards economic freedom and reinforces the central theme of adapting to and thriving after financial crises.

Year	Event	Personal Savings Rate Increase	Source
2007-2009	Great Recession	2.3 percentage points	IMF Working Papers Volume 2012 Issue 042
2020-2021	COVID-19 Pandemic	2.5 percentage points	Federal Reserve Economic Data

Changes in Personal Savings Rates During Economic Crises

MORTGAGE DEBT LEVELS POST-CRISIS

In the aftermath of the financial crisis, many families faced the daunting reality of precarious mortgage debt levels that had far-reaching implications for their overall financial stability. As homes lost significant value, countless homeowners found themselves underwater, unable to sell without incurring substantial losses. This period not only exemplified the fragility of homeownership but also highlighted the systemic failures in lending practices that contributed to the crisis. In contemporary contexts, understanding these past dynamics is crucial for current homeowners and prospective buyers alike, who are navigating the complexities of modernization in mortgage lending. By examining the stark statistics from the post-crisis era—such as the gradual decrease in mortgage debt relative to disposable income—one can appreciate the evolution of borrowing standards and the importance of financial literacy. Reflecting on these lessons encourages an active engagement with one's own mortgage situation, fostering an environment where financial responsibility is paramount.

As the memories of the last crisis linger, an array of personal stories emerges that emphasizes resilience and adaptability in the face of financial adversity. Families who emerged from the wreckage often sought to redefine their relationship with debt, assessing not just their mortgage obligations but also how those debts influenced their lifestyle choices and future aspirations. One family's experience demonstrated the transformative power of creating a budget that prioritized savings while managing monthly mortgage payments. Their journey illustrates the importance of a multi-faceted approach towards financial management—coupling disciplined spending with purposeful saving and investment strategies. When principles of the RICH Method 2.0 are applied, individuals can break free from the cycle of anxiety tethered to mortgage obligations and instead cultivate a sense of agency over their financial future, which in turn contributes to a healthier economy as more individuals invest in their communities.

Moving forward, there is a compelling call to action for individuals and families to engage more holistically with their mortgage debt levels and overall financial education. Recognizing the historical context and tangible impacts of prior economic downturns allows homebuyers to take deliberate steps toward informed decision-making. In practical terms, a useful exercise would involve participants listing their current mortgage terms alongside their total debt, followed by an exploration of different refinancing options that could alleviate burdensome rates. This proactive approach enables families to take ownership of their financial trajectories, fostering not only economic freedom but also community resilience against potential future crises. By encouraging discussions and sharing experiences, more individuals can empower themselves with knowledge, thereby improving not just their finances but also the collective economic health of society.

Year	Mortgage Debt (Trillions USD)
2008	10.7
2012	9.3
2019	9.1
2024	12.44

U.S. Household Mortgage Debt Levels Post-Crisis

LABOR MARKET TRENDS AND THEIR EFFECTS

Amid the fluctuating dynamics of today's economy, many find themselves reflecting on personal experiences that reveal larger labor market trends. A young entrepreneur shared how the pandemic shifted her business approach, leading her to pivot away from retail towards e-commerce. This shift mirrors broader structural changes in the labor market, where remote work and digital services have surged. According to recent labor statistics, sectors employing digital skills have outpaced traditional jobs, illustrating a clear demand for adaptive labor. These changes not only affect employment patterns but also highlight a vital need for financial literacy; workers must navigate new economic landscapes with a strategic mindset. The narrative encourages individuals to recognize their unique skills and areas for growth and transformation, emphasizing the urgency of embracing flexible skill sets that align with market demands. This recognition forms a cornerstone of the RICH Method 2.0, urging individuals to prepare for the economic realities that stem from evolving labor market trends.

As labor markets become increasingly competitive, many individuals are grappling with the effects of wage stagnation on their financial well-being. A family's story unveils the struggle of living paycheck to paycheck, overshadowed by rising living costs and inadequate wage growth. This scenario resonates with broader trends, as growth in hourly earnings has failed to keep pace with inflation for decades. The ripple effect of this stagnation extends beyond immediate financial pressure; it influences long-term savings behaviors and investment opportunities. The disconnect between earnings and living costs presents a stark reality—those who do not adapt may find it challenging to achieve economic freedom.

By understanding these labor market dynamics, readers can explore alternative income streams or skill enhancements that may yield higher pay. The narrative serves as a call to action for individuals to reconsider their approaches to earnings, urging them to invest in education and skills that promote financial resilience in light of wage stagnation.

Confronting the challenges posed by the shifting labor market also calls for strategic financial planning, particularly through the establishment of a robust safety net. A recent interview with a financial advisor revealed that many families overlook emergency savings during periods of wage deterioration. This oversight often leads to cascading financial troubles, as individuals are ill-prepared for unexpected expenses, such as job loss or health emergencies. Interestingly, effective budgeting and diligent savings can create that much needed buffer. By examining the savings behaviors of families who thrived during economic uncertainty, one can glean important lessons on prioritizing savings while managing daily expenditures. Integrating practical exercises into the RICH Method 2.0, individuals can create personalized saving plans to fortify their financial well-being in uncertain labor environments. In the end, cultivating a proactive approach not only mitigates immediate risks but also fosters a sustainable trajectory toward economic freedom, enabling families to navigate labor market upheavals with confidence.

Year	Agricultural Employment	Manufacturing Employment	Unemployment Rate	Labor Force Participation Rate	Average Hourly Earnings Growth
2021	2.6 millions	12.5 millions	4.2 %	62.4 %	3.9 %
2022	2.5 millions	12 millions	4 %	62 %	4 %
2023	2.4 millions	11.8 millions	3.8 %	61.8 %	4.2 %

Labor Market Trends and Effects in the United States

IV. INTRODUCING THE RICH METHOD 2.0

Adapting to post-crisis financial realities requires tangible strategies that can empower individuals to seize control over their economic futures. In this context, the RICH Method 2.0 emerges as more than just a financial framework; it stands as a beacon of hope for those disillusioned by economic downturns. The methods foundation rests on the principle of Reinvesting wisely, which encourages individuals to channel their savings into assets that yield long-term growth rather than succumbing to short-term whims. Consider the story of Maria, a single mother in Valencia, who used her modest savings to invest in a low-cost index fund. Instead of letting fear dictate her financial choices, she embraced calculated risks, illustrating that a strategic approach to reinvestment can lead to significant financial returns—a sentiment echoed by experts who stress the importance of patience and informed decision-making in achieving true economic freedom. To build on the gains from wise reinvestment, the RICH Method 2.0 advocates for Improving expense efficiency, a critical step that enables individuals and families to maximize their income potential. Realignment of spending habits can inevitably lead to significant savings, freeing up resources for investment and other wealth-building opportunities. Take, for instance, the Garcia family, who began tracking their monthly expenses rigorously. They discovered that a few unnecessary subscriptions and dining out less frequently could save them hundreds of dollars each month. These findings prompted discussions with financial advisors about reallocating those savings into their children's education fund. Such anecdotes not only emphasize the practical nature of the RICH Method but also highlight how modifying everyday spending can lay the groundwork for long-lasting financial stability and growth, encouraging readers to routinely assess their financial habits and embrace this vital step.

The RICH Method 2.0 focuses on creating a solid safety net, underscoring the importance of financial security in a world often riddled with uncertainties. The concept of a safety net is particularly illustrated through the experiences of Roberto, a former small business owner who lost his job during the recession. Recognizing the need for a financial cushion, he began establishing an emergency fund, utilizing the principles of the RICH Method to devise a meticulous savings plan. By prioritizing a three-to-six-month reserve of living expenses, he managed to weather the storm of unexpected financial hardships. This aspect of the RICH Method resonates with many individuals who feel vulnerable in a precarious job market, steering them toward practical action by stressing the necessity of foresight and resilience. By fostering habits that ensure a financial buffer, individuals can cultivate a mindset that embraces challenges as opportunities for growth, instilling confidence in their capability to navigate the economic landscape effectively.

OVERVIEW OF THE FIVE-STEP SYSTEM

In the journey toward financial empowerment, one can imagine a scenario where individuals struggle to make ends meet, continually balancing between critical expenses and mounting debts. This contrasted landscape serves as a backdrop for the introduction of the "RICH Method 2.0," a framework designed to foster economic freedom with a practical approach. The five-step system prompts users to Reinvest wisely, Improve expense efficiency, Create a solid safety net, and Harness purpose-driven saving. By focusing on these pivotal stages, individuals can systematically address their financial health, reducing reliance on debt and fostering a culture of informed spending. This dual focus on personal accountability and strategic foresight positions the system not merely as a reactive measure but as a proactive blueprint for sustainable financial management. Delving deeper into the first two steps—Reinvesting wisely and Improving expense efficiency—provides a clearer understanding of their transformative potential. Reinvesting wisely emphasizes the need for individuals to evaluate their financial assets critically, encouraging investments that yield not only monetary returns but also personal growth and security. Meanwhile, Improving expense efficiency tackles the common pitfalls of unchecked spending behaviors, urging users to analyze their expenditures critically. These steps promote awareness and mindfulness, allowing individuals to realign their financial habits toward more productive outcomes. As numerous success stories illustrate, families who embraced these practices experienced significant shifts in their financial landscape, cultivating a sense of agency over their resources and inspiring others in their communities to do the same.

Shifting focus to the latter stages of the five-step system, Creating a solid safety net and Harnessing purpose-driven saving reinforce the importance of emotional and strategic preparedness in the face of uncertainty. A solid safety net ensures that individuals are equipped to navigate unexpected challenges without reverting to debt, fostering resilience in times of crisis. In tandem, the act of Harnessing purpose-driven saving transforms the way individuals conceptualize their savings; saving ceases to be a mere afterthought and evolves into a targeted effort toward achieving specific goals. This dynamic interplay not only bolsters financial stability but also infuses individuals financial journeys with meaning. As readers engage with these steps, practical exercises encourage the continuous application of these principles, driving home the notion that economic freedom is an achievable reality, grounded in disciplined and thoughtful financial choices.

IMPORTANCE OF A STRUCTURED APPROACH

In the fumbling world of personal finance, where uncertainty often reigns supreme, the chaos of unstructured decision-making can lead individuals down a treacherous path of financial ruin. Many families find themselves grappling with the weight of excessive debt and inadequate savings, often due to a lack of a coherent strategy. A disciplined, structured approach can serve as a compass, guiding individuals toward financial coherence and empowerment. Consider a family of four who overcame significant credit card debt through meticulous budgeting, thereby underscoring the transformative power of a structured method. By consciously tracking their expenses, they identified recurring costs that could be slashed, enabling them to prioritize vital savings. Such a scenario illustrates that the thoughtful organization of financial priorities is not merely a luxury, but a necessity for achieving lasting economic stability, echoing the principles laid out in the RICH Method 2.0.

Delving deeper, the structured approach offers more than just relief from immediate challenges; it fosters a mindset of proactive financial engagement that can bear fruit in the long term. As families embrace intentionality in their financial habits, they gain a clearer understanding of their economic landscape. A mother, once overwhelmed by tuition payments and household expenses, shared how she redesigned her budgeting framework to account for her children's future education. Through diligence and a structured plan, she established a 529 plan, allowing her to alleviate future financial strains while empowering her children. This narrative brings to light a pivotal aspect of the RICH Method 2.0: the necessity of viewing finance through a future-oriented lens. Such perspectives cultivate disciplined saving, ultimately positioning families to weather economic storms with greater confidence and agility.

To truly internalize the lessons of structured financial management, transforming theory into actionable practices is crucial for lasting change. Families must not only absorb the concept of a methodical approach but also actively engage with it through tangible steps. The RICH Method 2.0 encourages participants to create weekly financial check-ins and set clear, achievable goals. By closely monitoring their progress, individuals can celebrate small victories, reinforcing a cycle of positive reinforcement. A young couple, for example, shared how their weekly financial meetings solidified their commitment to joint savings goals. The practice not only elevated their fiscal literacy but also strengthened their partnership. As this narrative concludes, it highlights the essence of the RICH Method 2.0: it is about creating a structured financial environment where economic freedom is not an elusive dream but an attainable reality nurtured through consistent, practical action. As readers consider their own economic pathways, they are invited to draft their financial action plans, paving the way toward a freer and more secure future.

HOW RICH METHOD 2.0 DIFFERS FROM TRADITIONAL METHODS

In a world still grappling with the aftershocks of the last financial crisis, many individuals find themselves revisiting their approach to personal finances. Traditional financial methods often emphasized savings accounts and high-interest returns, relying on outdated beliefs that overlook the complexities of modern economic realities. In contrast, the RICH Method 2.0 champions a more comprehensive approach, focusing on reinvesting in diverse income streams and adapting expenses strategically. Rather than relegating savings to stagnant accounts, this method encourages individuals to explore investment opportunities that are aligned with their personal values and long-term goals. By prioritizing active engagement with finances, RICH Method 2.0 recognizes the necessity of dynamic strategies —an important evolution from the past to help mitigate the risks of another economic downturn.

Simplifying the financial landscape is paramount for individuals trying to navigate the murky waters of economic instability. Traditional financial advice often left consumers feeling overwhelmed and uncertain, promoting a one-size-fits-all mentality that failed to consider the unique circumstances of each person or family. The RICH Method 2.0 addresses this deficiency by offering practical, relatable guidelines that encourage personal reflection and tailored strategies. Anecdotes from everyday families illustrate how comprehensive expense tracking and goal-oriented saving can cultivate a deeper understanding of one's financial habits. Instead of passive compliance with financial norms, individuals are inspired to actively dissect their spending patterns and identify areas of improvement. The method includes ongoing support through community engagement, offering a network of like-minded individuals striving for similar financial growth —an invaluable asset rarely found in traditional approaches. The power of the RICH Method 2.0 lies in its emphasis on cultivating a solid safety net while harnessing purpose-driven saving. Unlike the conventional model, which often prioritizes emergency funds without addressing their practical use, this method frames financial security as a launching pad for greater investment opportunities. Real-life success stories reveal how families, once overwhelmed by debt, transformed their mindsets by adopting deliberate practices that align with their financial aspirations. Engaging with professionals for personalized advice is encouraged, yet individuals are simultaneously empowered to take charge of their financial destinies. As this new paradigm takes hold, practical exercises accompanying the method ensure that users do not just learn financial principles but actively implement them. This foundational shift not only fosters economic freedom but also inspires a renewed sense of agency in one's financial journey.

V. REINVESTING WISELY

In the aftermath of the financial crisis, many individuals found themselves confronting the stark reality of financial instability. Imagine a young couple, struggling to recover from job loss and mounting student debt, making ends meet while yearning for a more secure future. This scenario is increasingly common, underscoring the importance of reinvesting wisely— not merely surviving your financial situation but actively seeking avenues for growth. By reinvesting savings into vehicles with higher returns, such as diversified mutual funds or real estate, individuals can leverage their resources to create wealth. The statistics are compelling: data from recent economic reports indicate a clear correlation between strategic reinvestment and improved financial resilience, with those who prioritize reinvestment averaging a significantly higher net worth than their counterparts. The takeaway for the average family is clear: with careful planning and informed choices, financial independence is within reach.

As we delve deeper into the practice of reinvesting wisely, personal narratives reveal the transformative power of informed financial decisions. Consider the story of Maria, a single mother who embraced systematic reinvestment after attending a financial literacy workshop. Initially hesitant, Maria learned to redirect her savings into low-cost index funds, demystifying the world of investments that once felt inaccessible. Her journey is a testament to the impact of education and confidence in financial decision-making, illustrating how small, consistent actions can lead to substantial gains over time. Marias story resonates with many; it highlights that reinvesting isn't limited to affluent individuals but is indeed a viable path for anyone committed to enhancing their financial health. Thus, individuals are encouraged to assess their own savings strategies and consider reallocating a portion towards investment opportunities tailored to their risk tolerance and financial goals.

The framework of the RICH Method 2.0 encapsulates the essence of financial empowerment through strategic reinvestment. To ensure that it resonates with a wide audience, readers can take actionable steps toward incorporating these principles into their lives. A practical exercise might include creating a monthly budget that identifies discretionary spending, fostering mindful expenditure while earmarking a specific percentage of income for investment. This hands-on approach not only cultivates discipline but allows individuals to track their reinvestment growth over time. By linking the act of reinvesting to the prospect of long-term financial freedom, participants can shift their mindset from immediate gratification to sustainable wealth creation. As families take these steps to reevaluate their financial habits, they become empowered to forge a path toward economic independence, transforming the lessons learned from past crises into a blueprint for future stability.

STRATEGIES FOR EFFECTIVE REINVESTMENT

In times of financial uncertainty, individuals often find themselves confronted with the daunting task of deciding how to allocate their limited resources. This decision-making process becomes particularly critical when considering reinvestment strategies, as the choices made can significantly influence long-term financial stability. A family might grapple with whether to funnel their savings into a high-yield savings account or invest in low-cost index funds. Insights from financial advisors highlight that diversification is key; by spreading investments across various asset classes, individuals not only mitigate risk but also harness growth potential. Real-life stories, such as that of a single mother who transformed her emergency savings into a growing investment portfolio, serve as powerful motivators. By actively engaging with their reinvestment strategies, families can adapt their financial plans to meet shifting economic realities, thereby paving a path toward greater economic freedom.

Reinvestment is not solely about choosing where to place funds; it encompasses understanding the cyclical nature of markets and personal finance. Educated reinvestment strategies involve analyzing economic indicators, such as interest rates and inflation, to determine the optimal timing for investing. When inflation rates are low, holding onto cash might yield value, but as rates rise, investing those funds becomes increasingly crucial. In interviews, retirees have recounted the importance of being proactive rather than reactive. By staying informed and seeking advice, they were able to avoid common pitfalls, such as emotional decision-making during market downturns. This perspective emphasizes that effective reinvestment is a dynamic process, requiring continuous learning and adaptation. By integrating these principles into everyday financial practices, individuals armed with knowledge are better positioned to seize opportunities and safeguard their financial futures.

Effectively reinvesting requires not just knowledge, but a commitment to continuous improvement. A practical exercise in developing a reinvestment strategy could involve creating a monthly budget to track discretionary spending, allowing for a clearer view of surplus funds available for reinvestment. This proactive approach can help individuals identify trends in their spending habits, thereby illuminating potential areas for reinvestment. A family might discover that cutting back on dining out allows them to reinvest in a robust retirement account. As personal finance stories illustrate, small but deliberate adjustments can snowball into significant financial changes. Relying on disciplined saving and strategic reinvestment not only promotes economic freedom but also empowers individuals to confront economic challenges head-on, transforming uncertainty into opportunity for prosperity.

IDENTIFYING HIGH-RETURN OPPORTUNITIES

Amidst the uncertainty that follows any economic upheaval, individuals often find themselves eyeing opportunities imbued with potential for high returns. Consider the story of Sarah, a single mother from Madrid, who leveraged the crisis by identifying undervalued properties in struggling neighborhoods. Conversations with local real estate agents revealed a pattern: homes that took a hit during the recession were now primed for significant value appreciation. Data supports this narrative, indicating that markets in recovery phases often yield remarkable returns for those who can see beyond the immediate vicissitudes of the economy. By embracing a forward-thinking approach, Sarah not only secured a stable living situation but also laid the groundwork for additional income through rental arrangements. As a gentle reminder, potential investors should start by analyzing their local markets—attending open houses, engaging with community networks, and scouring online listings—to uncover such hidden opportunities ripe for investment.

While the real estate sector often garners attention, high-return opportunities can also emerge from unexpected venues, such as small business investment. Take the case of Javier, an entrepreneur who pivoted his catering business into a meal prep service during the pandemic. His venture was propelled by data illustrating a rising consumer trend towards convenient, healthy eating options. By harnessing online marketplaces and social media platforms, he tapped into a growing clientele ready to embrace lifestyle changes that align with their newly defined priorities. Analysis of market demands, alongside agile adaptation, has been essential in distinguishing successful ventures from less viable ones. Aspiring entrepreneurs can proceed by conducting thorough market research, participating in local business associations, or seeking mentorship from seasoned professionals. Each step taken towards understanding market dynamics can create a powerful pathway to uncover profitable opportunities.

Identifying high-return avenues also requires a keen awareness of emerging technologies and consumer behaviors, especially in our increasingly digital world. The narrative of Raúl, a self-taught tech enthusiast, illustrates this perfectly; he recognized the skyrocketing demand for digital marketing services early in the crisis. Despite facing initial skepticism from family and friends, his commitment to the learning process allowed him to create a thriving online consultancy. Market analysis indicated that businesses were rapidly shifting their advertising strategies towards digital platforms, allowing Raúl to capitalize on this trend. To mirror his success, individuals must actively engage in continuous education, whether through online courses or industry webinars, equipping themselves with relevant skills that can translate into real-world profit-making potential. Reflection on these insights can guide aspiring investors and entrepreneurs in their journey towards financial independence as they harness the latest innovations to achieve high returns.

CASE STUDIES OF SUCCESSFUL REINVESTMENT

In the wake of the last recession, many families traversed the tumultuous landscape of depleted savings and rising debts. A notable case is that of the Martinez family, who, after losing their primary source of income, took a hard look at their financial practices. Initially overwhelmed by emergency expenses, they found themselves steeped in credit card debt. They decided to embrace the RICH Method 2.0, notably focusing on reinvesting wisely. By reallocating their limited resources toward further education and skills training, Mr. Martinez enhanced his employability, ultimately landing a more secure and higher-paying job within six months. This reinvestment not only alleviated their initial financial strain but also empowered them to view their circumstances through a lens of opportunity rather than just crisis—a critical shift that holds the potential to inspire others facing similar challenges.

As the Martinez family's story illustrates, successful reinvestment is not solely about recovering losses; it is about adopting a proactive mindset that transforms adversity into potential growth. In another compelling case, the Rodriguez family faced similar struggles but chose a different path centered around expense efficiency. They tackled their existing expenses head-on by renegotiating service contracts and switching to more cost-effective alternatives. The decision to downsize their living situation and embrace a shared vehicle model not only cut their monthly costs significantly but also augmented their savings—funds the family then strategically employed to invest in a small local business. Such real-life examples underscore the premise that mindfulness in spending can be just as powerful as active reinvestment, crafting a dual approach that fortifies financial resilience.

The narratives of the Martinez and Rodriguez families serve as beacons of possibility, demonstrating that the application of the RICH Method 2.0 can yield transformative results. Transitioning from crisis to opportunity requires not only strategic reinvestment but also a commitment to harnessing purpose-driven savings. Through the power of storytelling, these case studies challenge readers to reflect on their own financial practices. They illustrate that true economic freedom lies in recognizing the potential for growth within the confines of current situations. Hence, the call to action becomes clear: take stock of your financial habits, assess your reinvestment opportunities, and engage in weekly challenges aimed at building a more robust financial foundation. Consolidating insights from others' experiences accelerates progress toward personal financial empowerment.

VI. IMPROVING EXPENSE EFFICIENCY

In the wake of financial upheaval, many families found themselves grappling with more than just financial instability; they encountered the harsh reality of poor spending habits. Take, for instance, the story of the López family, who used to spend liberally on takeout meals and impromptu shopping sprees, leaving little room for savings. After attending a financial workshop, they implemented the RICH Method 2.0's focus on improving expense efficiency. By introducing a weekly budget and tracking their expenditures, they unearthed significant savings. Essential needs received priority, while discretionary spending was scrutinized. This not only alleviated their immediate financial strain but also fostered a culture of awareness regarding their money choices. Their experience reflects a broader trend: simple budgeting practices can empower families to regain control over their finances. The first step is identifying one recurring expense to scrutinize, which can be a powerful catalyst for sustainable financial change.

Notably, improving expense efficiency also involves leveraging technology, a factor particularly salient in today's digital age. Numerous applications offer easy tracking of expenses, allowing individuals to gain insights into their spending habits with considerable precision. This can be overwhelming, but the experience of the Martínez family illustrates how technology can promote expense awareness. They turned to a popular budgeting app and began categorizing not just their purchases, but determining which expenses could be reduced. They discovered that their subscription services exceeded what they actively used. By canceling unnecessary subscriptions and reallocating those funds towards savings, the Martínez family saw their monthly budget transform dramatically. Such digital tools turn an abstract concept into a tangible practice that demystifies personal finance. Readers are encouraged to download a budgeting app and set a goal to reduce one discretionary spending category this month.

The journey towards financial empowerment through improved expense efficiency can create ripples that extend beyond the household. When families adopt conscious spending habits, they cultivate a self-sustaining environment where financial literacy flourishes, particularly among younger generations. The success story of the Gonzalez family underscores this point. As they became more cost-conscious, their teenage daughter began managing her own allowance, learning invaluable skills in budgeting and saving. This positive feedback loop emphasizes that efficient spending isn't just about cutting costs; it's about fostering an understanding of financial responsibility. Families can serve as role models to one another, paving the way for broader community change. To reinforce this, individuals are encouraged to share their expense-saving strategies with friends and family, creating an informal support network that holds everyone accountable. As each household commits to improving expense efficiency, they contribute collectively to a culture of economic resilience.

ANALYZING EXPENSES FOR REDUCTION

Every month, countless families face the same dilemma: bills pile up, and income seems to vanish quicker than anticipated. This predicament often roots from a lack of understanding and analysis of personal expenses. The RICH Method 2.0 emphasizes the importance of dissecting one's spending habits as a foundational step toward financial freedom. By systematically cataloging monthly expenditures, individuals can identify unnecessary spending or recurring subscriptions that may no longer serve their goals. A remarkable instance is Claudia, a single mother from Madrid, whose unforeseen monthly expenses were reduced by 25% simply by eliminating redundant streaming services. Her story illustrates the potential for substantial savings through mindful examination of expenses. This practice not only curates a clearer financial picture but also instills a sense of empowerment, motivating families to take actionable steps towards economic independence. As a first exercise, start by tracking your expenses for a month to uncover areas ripe for reduction. Once individuals confront their spending patterns, the next step involves prioritizing and categorizing these expenses. A strategic analysis can help distinguish between essential, discretionary, and luxury items. Lucas and Maria, a couple grappling with student debt, initially lumped all expenses together, overlooking significant waste in categories like dining out and entertainment. By separating their expenses into meaningful categories, they identified that replacing a few restaurant outings with home-cooked meals saved them nearly €300 each month. This type of categorization is pivotal because it encourages families to reflect on which expenses align with their values and goals. The realization that money spent on non-essential items could be funneled into savings or debt reduction is an enlightening moment for many. To begin this categorization process, consider using a simple spreadsheet or app that allows you to visualize where your money goes each month.

In addition to categorization, seeking external perspectives can enhance understanding of expense patterns. Engaging with financial advisors or participating in community workshops can offer invaluable insights drawn from broader economic data and personal anecdotes. Javier, an entrepreneurial advisor, recently emphasized how those who shared their financial stories with peers reported a clearer grasp of their spending habits. Encouragingly, collaboration often leads to innovative solutions that might not have been considered otherwise. The social aspect of financial management cannot be underestimated: many families find motivation and accountability in discussing and comparing their expense-tracking successes with others. Consequently, forming or joining a community focused on financial education might be the key to unlocking new strategies for expense minimization. To foster this sense of community, challenge yourself to share your budgeting goals with a friend or family member, setting the stage for mutual learning and support.

TOOLS AND TECHNIQUES FOR BUDGETING

Imagine a young couple, newlywed and eager to build their future, sitting at their dining table, surrounded by stacks of receipts and bills. The weight of financial uncertainty often leads to anxiety and impulsive spending, yet this couple soon discovers the power of budgeting tools, like the zero-based budget. This method pushes them to allocate every dollar they earn to specific categories, ensuring nothing is left unaddressed. By understanding their income and expenses, they not only gain clarity but also cultivate a sense of control over their finances. This approach emphasizes why budgeting isn't just about restraint; it allows individuals to prioritize their goals amidst everyday needs. By implementing the zero-based budget, they notice a shift—a newfound awareness that not only mitigates stress but enables them to save consistently. The exercise here involves creating a zero-based budget for the next month, giving a tangible starting point to regain financial stability.

As they continue their budgeting journey, the couple explores the role of digital tools and apps designed to streamline financial management. Utilizing applications like Mint or YNAB (You Need A Budget), they find that these platforms offer an engaging way to track spending, set saving goals, and even sync with bank accounts for real-time updates. The immediate feedback from these tools fosters a daily habit of financial review, enhancing their understanding of where money flows in and out. The aspect of gamification inherent in these technologies makes budgeting less daunting and more achievable, especially for those reluctant to confront their spending habits. As user interviews reveal, many couples have reported significant debt reductions and improved saving rates simply by integrating these digital solutions. In closing, readers are encouraged to select one budgeting app that appeals to them and commit to using it daily for a week—transforming abstract financial goals into actionable measures.

While the couples newfound financial awareness empowers them, they ultimately realize the importance of budgeting as a continual process. This insight is reinforced by the effectiveness of the envelope system, where cash is allocated for specific expenses like groceries and entertainment, ensuring they stick to pre-determined limits. The tactile experience of handling cash fosters a deeper connection to their spending habits and prioritizes savings through visible reminders. Evidence suggests that physically separating funds for different purposes encourages more disciplined financial behavior. Their journey serves as a testament to the dual nature of budgeting as both a practical tool and a psychological framework. Each month, they can revisit and adjust their envelopes based on changing needs, reinforcing the adaptable nature of personal finance. As a challenge for readers, consider implementing an envelope system or its digital counterpart by designating a specific fund for discretionary spending, highlighting the power of tangible boundaries in achieving financial freedom.

REAL-LIFE EXAMPLES OF EXPENSE MANAGEMENT

Navigating the treacherous waters of personal finance can often feel overwhelming, particularly in the aftermath of a crisis when uncertainty runs high. A profound illustration of effective expense management can be found in the story of Maria, a single mother living in Madrid, who found herself grappling with significant credit card debt following the last recession. Implementing a meticulous budgeting strategy not only helped her regain control but also allowed her to reallocate funds towards a future savings goal. By categorizing her expenses—distinguishing between essentials and discretionary spending—Maria learned to cut back on non-essential items. In her case, this meant swapping dining out for home-cooked meals. Her journey, while distinctly personal, shines a light on a universal truth: precise expense tracking can transform financial chaos into clarity, paving the way for economic freedom.

Sharing Marias experience reveals a common thread in personal finance: the necessity of shifting mindset towards proactive expense management. Adam, a millennial entrepreneur, has adopted expense management practices that echo Marias journey but are tailored to his evolving lifestyle. After facing initial business struggles, he discovered the power of app-based tracking to monitor monthly expenditures against income. This newfound awareness pushed him to scrutinize recurring subscriptions and unnecessary business expenses, leading to a 30% decrease in overhead costs. He recognized the importance of aligning spending with both business goals and personal values—a principle that resonates strongly in today's entrepreneurial climate. Adam's story elucidates that effective expense management transcends mere budgeting; it encapsulates an ongoing commitment to long-term financial health and adaptability in a shifting economic landscape.

As individuals like Maria and Adam embrace the core tenets of the RICH Method 2.0, they underscore the practicality of expense management as a stepping stone toward broader economic resilience. Central to this method is the call to action: individuals must actively engage in refining their financial practices. A simple yet impactful exercise to consider involves creating a financial diary for one month, where readers document and categorize all expenses, small or large. This practice not only heightens awareness but also fosters a critical understanding of spending habits that might previously have gone unnoticed. In concluding their narratives, both Maria and Adam exemplify that the journey to financial freedom is less about rigid constraints and more about informed choices—each decision a step towards reclaiming control over ones economic destiny.

VII. CREATING A SOLID SAFETY NET

Imagine finding yourself at a crossroads, where a sudden job loss is just around the corner, catching you off guard. This scenario is all too familiar for many, especially during economic downturns. A solid safety net serves as a cushion against these unexpected shocks, providing a sense of security and stability. To build this safety net, individuals must assess their financial landscape and take proactive measures. Financial experts often recommend aiming for at least three to six months' worth of living expenses saved in an easily accessible account. This target is not arbitrary; it stems from the reality that unexpected expenses frequently arise, be it through health crises, home repairs, or job instability. Stories of families who faced such challenges reveal that those with an adequate safety net navigated crises more smoothly, allowing them to focus on solutions rather than solely on survival. Transitioning from awareness to action, many have experienced the immediate benefits of a well-structured emergency fund. Consider the case of a young couple who, despite their modest income, managed to save diligently over the course of three years. They chose to forgo luxury and, instead, prioritize their financial resilience. Their commitment paid off when one of them faced a sudden job loss during a downturn; the emergency fund not only preserved their living standards but also provided the couple with the breathing room to find a new job that aligned with their career goals. Such examples underline the essence of patience, discipline, and strategic planning in creating a safety net. It is crucial for readers to recognize that building this financial foundation is an ongoing process, not a one-time effort.

As we explore practical steps to establishing this safety net, one powerful recommendation is to automate savings. Implementing an automatic transfer to a designated savings account every month can eliminate the temptation to spend that money elsewhere. This method reflects a key principle: make saving easier than spending. The immediate reward may feel negligible, but over time, small contributions accumulate, leading to significant financial resilience. Keeping financial goals tangible and visual can further enhance motivation. Consider a family that created a visual savings tracker, marking their progress toward a specific fund. What started as a simple chart soon evolved into a source of pride and inspiration, effectively urging them to reach new financial goals. Readers are encouraged to reflect on their own savings strategies and to take a moment each month to assess their progress, allowing them to internalize the principle that financial freedom is built through consistent small steps.

IMPORTANCE OF EMERGENCY FUNDS

In the tumultuous world of personal finance, unexpected expenses can feel like murky waters threatening to drown your carefully laid plans. Consider the couple, Maria and Pedro, who, after years of saving, found themselves facing a sudden medical emergency. The shock of the hospital bill spiraled them into debt, highlighting the importance of a well-fortified emergency fund. Financial experts often emphasize that a safety net should ideally cover three to six months of living expenses. This practice not only provides peace of mind but serves as a crucial buffer during life's unpredictable events. Real-life stories like Maria and Pedro's offer a stark reminder that without this financial cushion, individuals may resort to high-interest debt options, which can lead to chronic financial instability. Instilling the discipline to prioritize emergency savings is not just wise—it's essential for long-term economic freedom.

Transitioning from a mere survival mindset to one of empowerment necessitates actionable steps, rooted in financial education. Imagine being in the driver's seat as you weather a storm rather than being tossed around at sea without a life preserver. This is where the RICH Method 2.0 emphasizes the creation of a solid safety net. Financial planners argue that successful budgeting should naturally account for unexpected expenses, thus incorporating an emergency fund into monthly financial planning must become non-negotiable. Yet the journey requires more than mere allocation; it involves cultivating a habit of setting aside a percentage of income—perhaps starting with 10%— that will gradually build up to a secure amount. Integrating such practices into everyday life transforms the narrative from reactive scrambling to proactive planning, enabling individuals to confidently navigate crises as they arise.

Reflecting on the socio-economic changes catalyzed by past crises illustrates a critical lesson: financial resilience is not accidental but an intentional choice. Consider diverse families across Spain, who, motivated by personal anecdotes and data-driven insights, have adopted emergency savings as a cornerstone of their financial health. The rise in the country's savings rate post-recession shows that economic awareness has evolved, with individuals recognizing that financial literacy directly correlates with their ability to withstand shocks. It's a clarion call for action; each reader must assess their current financial situation and commit to establishing their emergency fund. A practical exercise could involve creating a straightforward spreadsheet outlining essential expenses, as well as a realistic monthly savings goal. This exercise not only encourages accountability but also sets the stage for lasting financial independence, ultimately fostering a mindset shift toward security and self-sufficiency.

Percentage of Americans Without Emergency Fund	Source
42%	U.S. News 2025 Financial Wellness Survey
48%	Federal Reserve 2016 Economic Well-Being Report
36%	Federal Reserve 2021 Report
52.1%	National Financial Educators Council 2022 Survey

Statistics on Emergency Fund Preparedness in the United States

STRATEGIES FOR BUILDING A SAFETY NET

Everyday life presents numerous uncertainties, often compounding financial stress that lingers just beneath the surface. Savvy individuals recognize the importance of establishing a safety net, which serves not merely as a cushion against unforeseen events but also as a foundation for financial resilience. By prioritizing emergency savings, personal finance experts recommend setting aside at least three to six months' worth of essential living expenses. This pragmatic approach not only buffers against job loss or unexpected medical bills but also fosters a sense of security that encourages risk-taking, such as investing in education or entrepreneurial ventures. Stories abound of families who have turned financial calamity into opportunity by leveraging their safety net to explore new careers or start small businesses. As an effective exercise, consider analyzing your monthly expenditures to pinpoint areas where you can allocate funds towards building a dedicated emergency savings fund.

In addition to traditional savings, diversifying income streams is a key strategy for fortifying one's financial safety net. The recent economic fluctuations have revealed the vulnerabilities that come with relying solely on a paycheck, pushing families to seek alternative revenue sources. Informal surveys among industry professionals highlight the growing trend of side hustles, freelance endeavors, and passive income opportunities, such as rental income or dividend-earning investments. These additional income sources can not only supplement savings but also present pathways to achieving long-term financial goals. Personal anecdotes illustrate this point well, depicting individuals who transformed hobbies into profitable ventures—such as crafting or consulting—providing both a safety net and a fulfilling outlet. To embark on this journey, create a list of your skills and interests, assessing how they might be monetized in today's gig economy, thus laying the groundwork for a more robust and resilient financial future.

Effective budgeting serves as an indispensable tool in the overall strategy for building a safety net, ensuring that individuals can allocate resources wisely. Many people are surprised to discover how small changes in daily spending can accumulate significant savings over time. A structured budget highlights not only current spending patterns but also stresses the importance of separating needs from wants thereby empowering individuals to make informed financial decisions. The success stories of families who meticulously tracked expenses reveal inspiring transformations, often leading to healthier savings habits and proactive financial planning. As a practical exercise, consider utilizing a budgeting app or spreadsheet to track your expenditures weekly. Identify potential cuts or reallocations that will bolster your safety net, ultimately enhancing your preparedness for future economic fluctuations and fostering a sense of control over your financial landscape.

Year	Average Correct Answers	Comprehending Risk	Insuring
2017	49 %	37 %	47 %
2020	52 %	37 %	47 %

Financial Literacy and Preparedness Before the COVID-19 Crisis

TESTIMONIALS FROM FAMILIES WITH STRONG SAFETY NETS

Everyday life can often feel like a precarious balancing act, where any unexpected expense threatens to topple financial stability. This is a reality faced by many families, but those with robust safety nets tell a different story. Take, for example, the Garcia family, who transformed their approach to financial preparedness after experiencing a significant health emergency. With a comprehensive safety net that includes an emergency savings fund equivalent to six months of expenses, Garcia were able to navigate the crisis without derailing their long-term financial goals. They emphasize that cultivating such a safety net has not only provided peace of mind but also allowed them to make calculated decisions regarding investments and career changes. Their testimony underscores a key principle of the RICH Method 2.0, demonstrating the profound impact of foresight and planning on achieving economic freedom, urging families to prioritize building their own safety nets for future resilience.

In contrasting scenarios, other families highlight how the efficacy of a safety net can be traced directly to their financial education. The Rodriguez family, for example, learned valuable lessons in financial literacy through workshops and community programs designed to demystify budgeting and savings. Equipped with knowledge, they started with a small emergency fund, gradually building it over time, and now feel confident facing life's uncertainties. Their story resonates with many who find themselves overwhelmed by financial jargon and complicated principles. By sharing their journey, they hoist a flag of hope: anyone can reinforce their financial foundation with the right resources and commitment. Each family's experience echoes the overarching goal of the RICH Method 2.0: transforming financial awareness into actionable strategies that can empower families to create their own robust safety nets, ultimately paving the way for economic stability and growth.

The key takeaway from these powerful testimonials from families with strong safety nets is the necessity for proactive financial engagement and consistent practice. The Harringtons illustrate that constructing a safety net is not merely a one-time effort but a continuous journey. They advocate for setting incremental savings goals and utilizing budgeting apps to monitor their progress. By integrating a dedicated savings habit into their daily routine, the Harringtons have managed to strengthen their financial resilience against potential downturns. Their mantra is simple yet effective: slow and steady builds confidence. As families reflect on these insights, they are encouraged to consider practical exercises, such as setting aside a small percentage of each paycheck or participating in community financial workshops. These strategies not only reinforce the concept of a safety net but also stimulate a broader dialogue around financial education, accountability, and collective growth—an essential part of achieving true economic freedom in the aftermath of a crisis.

VIII. HARNESSING PURPOSE-DRIVEN SAVING

Navigating the tumultuous waters of personal finance often begins with introspection and a deep examination of one's motivations. While many view saving merely as an act of withholding expenditure, the rising wave of purpose-driven saving introduces a revolutionary mindset shift, transforming this chore into an empowering practice. Consider Maria, a single mother living in Valencia, who, after a financial setback during the last economic crisis, realized that her goal was not merely to save but to secure a stable future for her children. By identifying her purpose, she began to allocate her savings toward higher education funds and health care. This focused approach not only enhanced her savings rate but also filled her with a renewed sense of determination. Her story exemplifies how a clear purpose can invigorate saving practices, making them more purposeful and achievable; thus, it lays the groundwork for fostering long-term financial well-being.

Understanding the pressing need for efficient saving strategies gains momentum when we juxtapose emotional stories with hard data. Presently, the average savings rate in Spain hovers around 10%, a figure that pales in comparison to the recommended 20% for sustainable financial health. This discrepancy underscores a critical gap. Traditional savings methods often lack the motivating factors that can drive effective saving behavior. Engaging with the principles of purpose-driven saving illuminates a pathway where individuals not only shelter their financial resources but also empower their aspirations. By aligning savings with specific personal goals—such as homeownership or retirement—individuals like Juan, an aspiring entrepreneur from Madrid, have been able to significantly boost their financial discipline. The implementation of a tailored savings plan empowers people to view their financial responsibilities not as burdens, but as stepping stones toward realized dreams.

As we contemplate the overarching benefits of purpose-driven saving, practical steps toward integrating this concept into one's financial routine become paramount. The journey starts with a simple exercise: identifying personal values and translating them into saving goals. Create a vision board or a digital timeline that encapsulates specific objectives— whether they relate to family, travel, or personal growth. By visually mapping one's aspirations and connecting them directly to financial goals, individuals can harness a newfound motivation that transcends mere budgetary constraints. Just as Ana, a young professional, transformed her sporadic savings into a focused asset fund for her future business proposals, individuals can shift their perspective on saving. Engaging in this reflective practice not only supports robust financial habits but also fosters an enriching journey toward economic freedom, anchoring individuals firmly in control of their financial destiny.

DEFINING PURPOSE-DRIVEN SAVING

Imagine a young family living in a bustling city, juggling bills, childcare, and the myriad expenses of daily life. Amidst this chaos, the prospect of saving often seems daunting, if not impossible. Yet, purpose-driven saving can illuminate a path forward, replacing anxiety with intention. The essence of purpose-driven saving is rooted in understanding individual objectives—whether that's funding a family vacation, securing a child's education, or buying a first home. By defining these goals, families can create tailored savings plans that transform fleeting financial ambitions into tangible realities. This strategic approach not only fosters discipline but also cultivates a sense of ownership over ones financial future. As data reveals increasing savings rates among families who adopt goal-oriented strategies, the shift from aimless saving to purposeful allocation demonstrates the power of clarity in financial planning.

As families embark on their purpose-driven saving journey, relatable anecdotes often serve as powerful motivators. Consider Maria and José, a couple who turned their debt-ridden struggles into a flourishing financial narrative. By pinpointing their long-term goal of homeownership, they redirected their savings efforts from piecemeal contributions toward a dedicated fund for a down payment. Their regimented approach—combined with diligent tracking of savings and spending—enabled them to reach their goal faster than they initially anticipated. Maria notes that each time they contributed to their home fund, it reinforced their commitment, instilling motivation and excitement rather than dread over their finances. This narrative exemplifies the transformative impact of purpose-driven saving on a family's economic stability and sense of agency, further supporting the argument that financial goals breathe life into passive savings efforts.

To translate these insights into actionable steps, individuals must engage actively with their financial objectives. One effective exercise is to create a visual representation of savings goals—perhaps a vision board or a savings tracker app that displays progress. This tangible reminder of their aspirations keeps families connected to their financial purpose, fostering motivation through visualization. As they watch their savings grow, the emotional rewards reinforce their commitment, bridging the gap between aspiration and achievement. Incorporating periodic reviews of both progress and goals allows families to adjust their strategies based on shifting priorities or new insights. This cycle of setting, tracking, and revising goals not only strengthens discipline but also cultivates a proactive mindset that aligns perfectly with the principles of the RICH Method 2.0—transforming financial management from a chore into a purposeful journey toward economic freedom.

SETTING GOALS THAT MOTIVATE SAVING

Envisioning the future can be a powerful motivator when it comes to saving, and anchoring financial goals in tangible, relatable objectives can provide the necessary push to alter spending habits. Many individuals often find themselves adrift in their financial planning because their goals lack specificity. Instead of saying, "I want to save money," a person might specify, "I want to save $5,000 for a family vacation to Spain by next summer." This level of detail transforms an abstract intent into a concrete target. Recent studies reveal that people who set specific financial goals are generally more likely to succeed in their savings endeavors. The clarity provided through particular aspirations not only enhances motivation but also sets the stage for measurable progress, inviting individuals to regularly review their achievements and adapt their strategies where necessary. As a practical exercise, readers should draft their specific financial goals and break them down into actionable monthly savings plans. Beyond monetary targets, connecting financial goals to personal values can create a potent drive for savings. Individuals often find themselves passionate about causes, whether that entails supporting a child's education, affording a home, or traveling to heal from a longstanding personal setback. By placing financial targets in a broader context of personal significance, the drive to save intensifies, transforming saving from a mere obligation into an inspiring journey toward fulfilling ones dreams. Consider the story of Jenna, a mother who struggled to save until she decided her primary goal was to fund her daughters college education. This revelation reshaped her financial landscape and infused her savings strategy with renewed vigor. The emotional weight behind such goals often fuels a commitment that mere numbers cannot replicate. Readers are encouraged to reflect on their own values and reframe their financial aspirations to align with what truly matters to them, thereby enhancing their motivation to save.

Breaking down ambitious financial goals into manageable steps allows individuals to build a sense of accomplishment that reinforces the desire to continue saving. Initial setbacks can derail even the most determined savers; however, a strategy involving small, incremental objectives acts as a foundational approach to avoiding discouragement. If the ultimate aim is to save $15,000 for a home down payment, starting with a quarterly goal of saving $1,250 can make the larger target seem more achievable and less daunting. Achieving these smaller milestones leads to psychological wins that bolster confidence and commitment to the larger goal. Often, successful savers express that celebrating these tiny victories fosters a rewarding experience that makes the entire process enjoyable, rather than burdensome. As a final action step, readers should establish their own milestones and commit to celebrating each achievement, no matter how minor, reinforcing a culture of success in their financial journeys.

SUCCESS STORIES OF PURPOSE-DRIVEN SAVERS

The journey to financial independence often begins with a single realization: purposeful savings can lead to meaningful change. For many individuals and families, this understanding sparked transformative journeys toward economic stability. Consider the story of Maria and Joaquin, a couple who faced mounting debt after the recent economic downturn. With a workforce that had become unpredictable, they decided enough was enough. They implemented a saving approach tailored to their goals of homeownership and funding their children's education. By committing to a detailed budget that prioritized saving based on their unique values, Maria and Joaquin paid down their debt significantly, achieving a 20% reduction within a year. This realignment of financial priorities transformed not just their bank accounts but also their perspective on what it means to live with intention. Their experience serves as an inspiration, reminding us that deliberate action in savings can navigate us through financial challenges, promoting prosperity amid uncertainty. As individuals tap into their financial journeys, the stories of others illustrate the power of community and shared experiences. Take, for example, the Ramirez family, who turned to personal finance workshops offered at their local community center. They found not only practical knowledge but also encouragement from peers who share similar financial aspirations. Learning how to prioritize needs over wants reshaped their spending patterns, leading them to save actively for an emergency fund. Their results were nothing short of remarkable; within six months, they secured three months' worth of expenses, building a safety net that bolstered their confidence. By engaging in dialogues around finance, Ramirez tapped into the collective wisdom within their community, reinforcing the principle that saving is both a personal and collective journey. This narrative underscores the essential theme of support and education in moving toward economic freedom, illustrating how purposeful savings can be greatly enhanced by shared knowledge and motivation.

While personal finance is often viewed as an individual endeavor, it becomes significantly clearer when cross-referencing data to real-life experiences. With rising savings rates postcrisis showing a shift in consumer priorities, purpose-driven savers are paving the way for an economic revival. The case of Daniel, a young entrepreneur who committed to a saving driven lifestyle while launching his startup, exemplifies this shift. By relying on precise financial planning and a commitment to reinvesting profits back into his venture, he not only stabilized his business but also built substantial savings. Daniel's experience emphasizes that the intersection of conscious saving and judicious investment can yield impressive results. As readers reflect on such stories, they are encouraged to analyze their own financial habits against reliable data, learning that purposeful saving is less about sacrifice and more about crafting a future aligned with their deepest values. Now is the time for individuals to take strategic actions—setting clear, measurable savings goals can foster not only personal growth but lasting financial freedom.

IX. THE ROLE OF FINANCIAL EDUCATION

A significant gap often separates financial literacy from practical application, leaving many individuals ill-equipped to navigate their economic realities. This disconnect frequently manifests as poor decision-making in budgeting, savings, and investment, which only exacerbates the stress and uncertainty surrounding personal finances. Take, for instance, the story of a young couple, Jamie and Alex, who found themselves drowning in credit card debt after relying on impulsive spending habits rather than informed financial strategies. Their once stable financial situation eroded rapidly, prompting them to seek guidance. This experience is emblematic of the repercussions that arise from inadequate financial education. Research shows that individuals who engage in financial education initiatives consistently make better financial decisions, illustrating that empowering individuals with knowledge not only fosters personal accountability but also cultivates a greater awareness of the long-term impact of their choices. Empowering oneself through financial education emerges as not just important, but essential for achieving sustainable economic freedom.

While traditional education systems often overlook practical financial skills, the reality is that individual behavior in the realm of finance largely dictates one's economic trajectory. For many, like Jamie and Alex, the turning point arrived in the form of a community workshop that emphasized the fundamentals of personal finance, such as budgeting and debt management. This hands-on training illuminated concepts that had previously seemed abstract or unapproachable. Data indicate that financial education programs can lead to more diligent savings practices and lower debt levels, showcasing a correlation between knowledge acquisition and economic stability. Relatable anecdotes told by successful financial advisors, who themselves faced similar challenges, serve to transform daunting information into actionable advice. By prioritizing financial education, individuals are given the tools and the confidence needed to tackle real-world financial challenges. Thus, embracing education becomes a vital foundation for navigating post-crisis financial landscapes, as evidenced by the successes of those who have applied newfound knowledge. The pivotal role of financial education cannot be overstated; it serves as the backbone of the RICH Method 2.0. As families learn to reinvest wisely, improve their expense efficiency, create a solid safety net, and harness purpose-driven saving, they chart a new course toward economic freedom. Consider the practical exercise of creating a personal budget, where participants turn theoretical knowledge into motivational action. By applying structured templates for tracking income and expenses, and incorporating their values into saving strategies, individuals learn to visualize their financial future more clearly. This integration of education into daily life encourages a shift in mindset from reactive to proactive financial management. Strides toward economic freedom hinge not merely on acquiring financial knowledge but effectively internalizing it through consistent practice. As individuals implement the principles of the RICH Method 2.0, they transform their financial realities, reinforcing the indispensable connection between education, financial empowerment, and lasting economic stability.

IMPORTANCE OF CONTINUOUS LEARNING

Picture a young woman, Ana, who faced a financial upheaval during the last recession. With her savings depleted and job security a distant memory, she quickly recognized the importance of continuous learning in navigating turbulent economic waters. Ana began devouring personal finance books, attending workshops, and engaging with online courses that deepened her understanding of budgeting, investing, and managing debt. This shift not only enhanced her financial literacy but also equipped her with practical tools that proved crucial in her journey towards stability. The labor market is evolving rapidly, and those who commit to lifelong learning are positioning themselves to thrive rather than merely survive. By adopting a mindset of constant growth, individuals can avoid common pitfalls that lead to precarious financial situations. Continuous learning empowers people like Ana to adapt to shifting circumstances, ensuring they are not caught off-guard when economic challenges arise.

As we dissect Anas journey, it becomes clear that continuous learning is not merely ancillary; it is integral to long-term financial resilience. Hard data underscores this necessity: studies indicate that individuals actively engaged in learning about finance are more likely to achieve and maintain economic stability compared to their less-informed counterparts. By staying informed about trends such as changes in interest rates or shifts in the job market, one can make proactive decisions that safeguard financial well-being. A family that adopts a habit of understanding their spending patterns and seeks out educational resources can reallocate funds more effectively, move toward savings goals more confidently, and respond to economic changes with agility. Thus, it is essential not only to absorb information but also to apply it in real-world scenarios. When families commit to ongoing education, they fundamentally alter their relationship with money and, importantly, their ability to influence financial outcomes.

The journey of continuous learning culminates in empowerment—the ability to take informed action toward financial independence. By incorporating insights from personal experiences and empirical research, individuals can construct a robust financial framework that withstands economic turbulence. Consider this practical exercise: set aside one day each month dedicated solely to learning about personal finance, whether through podcasts, webinars, or reading. Create actionable goals based on what you discover that align with the RICH Method 2.0 components—Reinvesting, Improving efficiency, Creating a safety net, and Harnessing purpose. This commitment to learning can transform anxiety into knowledge, fear into strategy, and uncertainty into financial freedom. The cycle of education and practice not only fosters economic empowerment but also inspires others within the community to embark on their paths toward financial literacy and self-sufficiency, enhancing collective resilience amid change.

RESOURCES FOR FINANCIAL EDUCATION

Imagine a family sitting around the kitchen table, sifting through bills and wondering how they got to this point. This scenario mirrors the realities faced by many post-recession, as traditional education often glosses over essential financial skills. Resources for financial education must evolve beyond passive learning to engaging, practical formats. Online platforms have emerged as powerful tools, offering a variety of courses ranging from budgeting basics to complex investment strategies. Websites like Coursera or Khan Academy provide structured learning paths that cater to different skill levels, allowing users to revisit concepts at their own pace. Community workshops can bridge the gap between digital and personal engagement, enabling individuals to share experiences and strategies. By tapping into diverse resources—both technological and personal—families can cultivate a stronger financial foundation, ensuring they learn the lessons that crisis exposed. Setting aside dedicated time each week to explore a new resource can transform passive knowledge into actionable skills.

Picture an empowered mother explaining to her teenage son the significance of saving for emergencies. Real-life anecdotes like this illustrate the profound influence that active, hands-on financial education can have on the younger generation. Incorporating interactive features, such as simulation games and role-playing scenarios, into financial education strengthens understanding and retention. Interactive budgeting apps now exist that enable users to visualize their expenses in real time, offering a clearer picture of their financial health and encouraging responsible choices. Parents and guardians can become life coaches in financial literacy, imparting wisdom they have learned from trial and error. Engaging with children through budgeting exercises or simulated saving goals not only provides education but also fosters open discussions about money management. By promoting these educational strategies at home, families can encourage a culture of financial literacy, instilling habits that empower future generations to navigate financial challenges confidently.

As the dust settles from the financial crisis, it becomes essential for individuals to harness available resources for ongoing education. Local libraries and community centers frequently host workshops led by financial advisors that cover practical topics like retirement planning and debt management. These face-to-face interactions can demystify complex concepts and motivate hesitant individuals to take charge of their finances. Social media platforms are beginning to play a unique role in spreading financial knowledge, where influencers educate audiences about budgeting tips, investment opportunities, and mindset shifts. Engaging with communities on platforms such as Reddit or Facebook not only facilitates peer support but also encourages accountability among participants. Creating a practice of sharing financial tips with friends or within social circles can further solidify learning, transforming education into a collaborative effort. To harness these evolving resources effectively, consider setting a goal to attend one seminar or workshop monthly to build knowledge and foster a supportive financial network.

IMPACT OF EDUCATION ON FINANCIAL DECISIONS

In the aftermath of economic turbulence, many individuals find themselves grappling with financial uncertainty, often drawing inspiration from personal narratives that highlight the importance of education in shaping financial decisions. The reality is that financial literacy does not merely equip individuals with knowledge; it empowers them to navigate a myriad of choices more effectively. When families are faced with mounting debts or the complexities of investment, those with a solid educational foundation tend to make informed decisions that mitigate risks and foster long-term stability. A single mother from a working-class background who learned basic financial principles through community workshops showcased how budgeting and saving strategies transformed her family's economic outlook. She now invests in her children's education, reinforcing the idea that education catalyzes positive financial behaviors that can be passed down through generations. Turning our focus to the hard data, studies suggest that individuals with higher levels of education are more likely to engage in strategic financial planning, such as retirement savings and investment diversification. This correlation between education and financial decision-making is not coincidental; those with advanced financial literacy exhibit greater confidence in navigating economic adversities and opportunities. A graduate in financial management may be more inclined to seek out diverse investment portfolios, while those without such knowledge often default to underperforming savings accounts or high interest loans. Anecdotal evidence from interviews with financial advisors reveals that educated clients are more proactive in managing their financial health, leading to improved outcomes and greater economic freedom. This is not to discount the challenges faced by less-educated individuals, but rather to underline that the educational divide creates disparities in financial competence that can be detrimental in times of crisis.

As we consider the implications of these insights, it becomes clear that education serves as a vital cornerstone for financial empowerment and decision-making prowess. The question that arises, then, is how to bridge these educational gaps in financial literacy, especially in vulnerable populations. Initiatives geared toward enhancing access to financial education can play an instrumental role in reshaping how families engage with their finances. One practical avenue might be community-based programs offering workshops or training that stimulate an interest in personal finance. Participants in such programs can start incorporating the lessons learned into their daily lives, fostering healthier financial habits. To encourage this, individuals might be challenged to draft a personal financial plan by the week's end, translating newfound knowledge into actionable steps aimed at securing their economic future. Through education, families can not only recover from financial setbacks but also build a resilient foundation for lasting economic freedom.

Study	Findings
The Effect of Personal Finance Education on The Financial Knowledge, Attitudes and Behavior of University Students in Indonesia	A 14-week personal finance course significantly improved financial knowledge among university students, but did not significantly affect financial attitudes or behaviors. Family financial socialization was a key driver of financial knowledge, attitudes, and behaviors.
Why Do Financially Illiterate Students Perceive Lower Education Returns? Evidence From a Survey in Rural China	Financially literate students have a more accurate perception of the returns to education, leading to better educational investment decisions.
Financial education affects financial knowledge and downstream behaviors	Randomized controlled trials indicate that financial education positively impacts financial knowledge and behaviors.
The effect of financial education on students' consumer choices: Evidence from a randomized experiment	Financial education increased students' financial literacy but did not significantly influence their consumer choices.
Quantifying the Causal Effect of Financial Literacy Courses on Financial Health	Financial literacy education has a significant positive effect on financial health, as measured by a composite score of financial health and distress metrics.

Impact of Education on Financial Decisions

X. INTERVIEWS WITH FINANCIAL ADVISORS

Navigating the aftermath of a financial crisis requires more than just understanding numbers; it demands an integration of lived experiences and professional insight. During interviews with financial advisors, common themes emerged that resonate deeply with families striving for economic freedom. One advisor recounted helping a family grappling with their home mortgage, emphasizing that many individuals tend to prioritize consumer spending over pivotal long-term investments. This approach often leads to a cycle of debt that stifles financial growth. Instead, the advisor recommended a strategy focused on the present and future, urging families to reevaluate their spending habits. The juxtaposition of this advice against the backdrop of rising mortgage debt levels in Spain serves as a poignant reminder: achieving financial stability starts with informed decision-making that aligns with one's fundamental financial goals. By embracing these insights, families can begin to reconstruct a financially sustainable future, grounded in prudent choices and awareness.

As the conversation evolved, the advisors shed light on the significance of improving expense efficiency. Personal stories shared by clients illustrated the stark differences between those who diligently monitored their expenditures and those who adopted a more laissez-faire attitude. One couple described how a simple exercise of itemizing their monthly costs illuminated unnecessary subscriptions draining their budget. They recounted the empowering moment of reallocating those funds toward savings, effectively reigniting their long-forgotten financial ambitions. The advisors consistently highlighted that a critical component of the RICH Method 2.0 involves this active engagement with one's finances. By recognizing and adjusting poor spending habits, individuals can more effectively allocate resources that bolster their economic safety nets. This insight points to a fundamental exercise: encourage readers to track their expenses for a month, illuminating the path toward financial efficiency and a clearer understanding of their monetary landscape. The advisors also placed significant emphasis on creating a solid safety net, particularly in light of lessons learned from the recent economic downturn. Their emphasis on proactive financial planning stood out during discussions, as they shared the narratives of clients who had not initially prioritized savings. One interviewee, who once faced unexpected medical bills, underscored the relief experienced after establishing a modest emergency fund. Such anecdotes strengthen the RICH Method's call to harness purpose-driven saving; advisors encourage individuals to set tangible savings goals tied to both immediate needs and future aspirations. This dual approach allows families not only to weather financial storms but also to pursue long-term growth with confidence. Closing the conversation, advisors recommended a practical step: challenge readers to establish an emergency fund that covers three to six months of living expenses, reinforcing the notion that preparedness transforms fear into agency in the face of uncertainty.

INSIGHTS FROM INDUSTRY EXPERTS

As individuals claw their way back from economic hardship, the voices of industry experts provide invaluable guidance. One financial advisor recently recounted how a family, drowning in debt due to past overspending, made a decisive pivot toward financial literacy. Through structured budgeting sessions and targeted savings plans, they reclaimed their financial health, demonstrating that the first step to recovery is often the hardest. Yet, data underscores that many continue to falter in this area; research indicates that a significant portion of the population lacks basic financial knowledge. Insights from experts confirm that understanding the foundation of personal finance is crucial for breaking the cycle of debt and fostering economic freedom. As individuals build their capacity for sound financial decision-making, they follow in the footsteps of those who overcame their struggles, making education a cornerstone of their journey towards financial stability.

Moving toward real-world applications, industry experts highlight the critical importance of efficient expense management. During a recent webinar, a renowned economist discussed how even small adjustments in spending habits can lead to substantial savings over time. One participant shared their experience of identifying recurring unnecessary expenses, like subscription services that went unnoticed. This revelation propelled them to reevaluate their priorities, leading to a more conscientious approach to spending. The accompanying data demonstrates that even a 10% reduction in discretionary spending can result in significant annual savings, proving that awareness catalyzes change. Experts stress that developing a savings mindset is imperative, as it lays the foundation for future investments. By embracing practical budgeting strategies and identifying potential savings, individuals can take control of their finances and work toward achieving their long-term economic goals.

At the heart of financial resilience lies the concept of a safety net—an idea championed by experts as essential in turbulent times. One financial planner shared a compelling success story of a small business owner who cultivated a robust emergency fund following a financial setback. This proactive approach not only shielded them during unforeseen circumstances but also allowed for strategic business investments when opportunities arose. Current insights reveal that households with three to six months' worth of expenses saved report higher confidence in weathering economic challenges. The concept of purpose driven saving also emerged as a transformative practice; individuals are encouraged to align their savings goals with personal values, enhancing motivation and commitment. Emphasizing the importance of establishing a safety net through deliberate saving contributes to the overarching narrative of the RICH Method 2.0. Readers are invited to begin this journey by assessing their emergency fund status, thereby taking a tangible step toward building economic security.

COMMON ADVICE FOR POST-CRISIS RECOVERY

Navigating the aftermath of a crisis can feel daunting, especially when faced with the financial shockwaves that often follow. Individuals and families commonly grapple with uncertainty as they assess the damage and plot a path to recovery. This situation calls for a methodical approach, drawing on principles that have proven effective in prior downturns. Common advice emphasizes the importance of reassessing financial priorities and adopting a more disciplined budgeting strategy. Anecdotes from families who took control of their finances after the last recession reveal a strikingly similar theme: a renewed commitment to understanding their spending habits. As one single mother recounted, reallocating her budget from non-essentials to savings transformed her outlook on financial adversity. This realignment fosters not only resilience but also empowers individuals to establish a detailed financial plan, which serves as a roadmap to recovery.

In practical application, the mantra of living within one's means emerges as a cornerstone for post-crisis recovery. The data illustrates a correlation between disciplined saving rates and long-term economic stability. Those who adopted stringent budgeting practices often reported a significant decrease in stress related to their financial situations. Real life examples echo this sentiment, as many families who previously endured crippling debt found relief through meticulous tracking of their expenditures. It's vital to build an awareness of one's spending habits, which allows individuals to strike a balance between necessity and luxury. Combining this insight with the practice of creating an emergency fund encourages a proactive mindset to address unforeseen challenges that may arise in the future. To that end, individuals can begin this journey by setting a monthly financial tracking goal, helping to foster accountability and create healthy spending habits.

Establishing a solid safety net is another critical aspect of post-crisis recovery, one that significantly influences economic freedom. During interviews with financial advisors, a recurring theme centered on the necessity of preparing for contingencies, whether they involve job loss or unexpected medical expenses. Families who successfully navigated the recent economic turbulence frequently cited their financial buffers as vital to their well-being. They often emphasized the sense of empowerment that comes from knowing they have a fallback plan. The establishment of a sufficient savings buffer inspires long-term confidence and diminishes the fear paralyzing many in the wake of financial crisis. Encouraging readers to reflect on their current safety nets kicks off an essential financial exercise: identifying areas where improvement is necessary. This exercise offers a practical blueprint to fortify defenses against future fiscal turmoil while providing peace of mind that accumulates through well-planned financial strategies.

STRATEGIES RECOMMENDED BY ADVISORS

In the wake of recent economic turbulence, individuals face a compelling need to reassess their financial strategies. Financial advisors have emphasized that establishing a practical and responsive budgeting system is crucial for navigating financial uncertainties. Consider a working couple who found themselves deeply in debt after unexpected home repairs. By employing a zero-based budgeting approach, they allocated every dollar to specific expenses, ensuring no funds went unmonitored. This strategy illuminated their spending habits and identified unnecessary subscriptions, ultimately enabling them to pay off a significant portion of their debt within months. Advisors recommend that such methods not only foster accountability but also instill a sense of control over ones finances. As household expenses fluctuate, creating a flexible yet structured budget can cushion against unforeseen challenges. As a practical exercise, readers are encouraged to assess their monthly expenditures and categorize them into necessary and discretionary spending, exploring opportunities to trim unnecessary outflows.

Another pivotal strategy underscored by financial advisors involves reinvesting savings into high-yield accounts or diversified portfolios. Amidst market volatility, the value of remaining adaptable and informed about investment vehicles cannot be overstated. Take, for instance, a single mothers journey towards financial freedom after learning about index funds and mutual investments during a community workshop. She began small, gradually reallocating her savings into a diversified portfolio, which not only yielded higher returns than her previous bank account but also instilled confidence in her financial acumen. Advisors note that understanding the risks and rewards associated with different investment strategies can significantly enhance ones financial trajectory. By doing so, individuals not only work towards wealth accumulation but also cultivate a mindset geared towards long-term growth. As an exercise, readers should research available investment options and reflect on which align best with their financial goals, taking actionable steps to begin diversifying.

Establishing a robust emergency fund remains a cornerstone of financial resilience and a key recommendation from advisors navigating the landscape of economic uncertainty. By creating a safety net that covers three to six months of living expenses, individuals can better withstand unexpected setbacks without resorting to credit accumulation. Picture a freelancer who faced a sudden dip in projects during a recession. With a dedicated emergency fund, she managed to sustain her living expenses while seeking new clients, demonstrating how proactive financial planning can alleviate immediate stress. Advisors advocate that setting aside even small amounts regularly can accumulate over time and significantly bolster ones financial stability. Encouraging readers to automate their savings through direct deposits or scheduled transfers can further ensure this fund grows consistently. As a practical exercise, individuals should assess their current savings strategy and set a target amount for their emergency fund, paving the way towards economic freedom in the face of future crises.

XI. SUCCESS STORIES OF ENTREPRENEURS

Every morning, thousands of individuals wake up eager to chase their dreams and improve their financial circumstances. For many, entrepreneurship serves as a viable path to economic freedom, especially in the aftermath of a crisis that disrupted traditional employment patterns. Notably, one entrepreneur turned a side hustle into a thriving online business after losing a stable job during the recession. This shift not only provided financial respite but also illuminated the importance of adaptability in a volatile marketplace. While statistics reveal that nearly half of small businesses fail within five years, those who persevere and pivot their strategies often find hidden opportunities. Such narratives underline the essence of the RICH Method 2.0, which encourages individuals to embrace financial reinvestment and efficiency. As we reflect on these success stories, readers are invited to assess their own skills and interests, and explore how a side venture might serve as a springboard to greater economic independence. Transitioning from employee to entrepreneur can be fraught with uncertainties, but the stories of those who have successfully navigated this path provide both inspiration and practical lessons. By harnessing a purpose-driven approach to saving and investment, many have transformed their fledgling businesses into sustainable income sources. One relatable example is that of a former teacher who launched an online educational platform, utilizing her expertise to generate revenue while catering to a burgeoning market. This not only provided her with financial stability, but also ensured that her work remained aligned with her passion for education. Success in such ventures often hinges on improving expense efficiency and understanding market demands. Each triumph is a reminder that financial literacy and strategic planning, central tenets of the RICH

Method 2.0, empower individuals to navigate their entrepreneurial journeys. Readers are encouraged to evaluate their budget allocations, identifying areas ripe for investment in potential business pursuits. The notion of success in entrepreneurship, especially in a post-crisis landscape, is not solely defined by financial gain but also by the resilience and growth experienced along the way. Personal stories highlight this journey, emphasizing how entrepreneurs have effectively overcome barriers such as market saturation and changing consumer behaviors. A local bakery that struggled to survive initially redefined its business model by focusing on community engagement and sustainability, attracting a loyal customer base invested in ethical consumption. Their story is a vivid illustration of the RICH Method 2.0s call for harnessing purpose-driven strategies that resonate with consumer values. Having a clear vision while maintaining financial prudence allows entrepreneurs to cultivate a strong foundation. Aspiring business owners are thus encouraged to create a roadmap, defining their objectives and aligning them with practical steps that lead toward sustained financial growth and stability.

Stadistic	Value
Percentage of new businesses failing within the first two years	20%
Percentage of new businesses failing within five years	45%
Percentage of new businesses failing within ten years	65%
Percentage of businesses failing due to lack of market need	42%
Percentage of businesses failing due to running out of cash	29%
Percentage of businesses failing due to not having the right team	23%
Percentage of businesses failing due to being out-competed	19%
Percentage of businesses failing due to pricing and cost issues	18%
Percentage of successful entrepreneurs who have mentorship or advisers	82%
Percentage of high-growth small businesses leveraging technology for growth	74%
Percentage of entrepreneurs who write formal plans and are more likely to achieve viability	16%
Average revenue for small businesses in the United States	$3.6 million
Percentage of small businesses investing in social media marketing to grow their business	61%

Entrepreneurship Success and Failure Statistics

OVERCOMING RISK AVERSION

When confronting financial uncertainties, individuals often succumb to an instinctual reluctance to embrace risk, a behavior that can critically undermine their economic potential. Consider a young couple who, after weathering the turmoil of job losses during the last recession, hesitates to invest in stocks despite a favorable market rebound. Their wariness stems not from a lack of capability but from deeply ingrained fear—fear of repeating past mistakes, fear of loss, and fear of the unknown. Yet, as demonstrated in interviews with successful financial advisors, overcoming such trepidation is not only feasible but necessary for long-term economic freedom. They emphasize that informed risk-taking, bolstered by meticulous financial planning, can yield significant returns. As illustrated through this couple's journey and similar stories, gradually empowering oneself to take calculated risks can transform both mindset and financial trajectory. Adopting a proactive approach to risk involves re-evaluating one's understanding of financial stability and growth opportunities. Data from recent studies suggest that individuals who embrace risk intentionally—such as diversifying their investment portfolios or exploring entrepreneurial ventures—often emerge ahead in today's dynamic economy. This revelation resonates with numerous anecdotal accounts from families who applied the RICH Method 2.0, shifting their perception of risk from a potential downfall to a pathway for growth. One family's decisive moment came when they transformed their side gig into a fulltime venture, initially faced with the same fears of instability that most encounter. With insights gathered from interviews, they learned that timely risk management led to not just financial resilience, but also personal development. For those looking to build wealth, reframing financial risk as a stepping stone rather than an obstacle becomes critical.

To translate this conceptual shift into actionable steps, its essential to create a structured plan that gradually integrates risk into one's financial life. A practical exercise could involve setting aside a small portion of one's income each month for experimentation—whether in stocks, index funds, or new business ideas—while maintaining an emergency fund. By taking small, measured risks, individuals can cultivate a more confident approach to their financial future. This method allows room for the inevitable learning curve that accompanies any new venture, reinforcing the understanding that not all risks result in loss. Drawing from real cases, families who implemented this strategy reported not just improved financial situations but enhanced peace of mind. As readers engage with their personal finances, the call to action remains clear: embrace the discomfort of risk, and let it propel you toward a more economically liberated life.

INNOVATIVE BUSINESS STRATEGIES POST-CRISIS

As businesses emerged from the shadows of the recent financial crisis, many faced a stark reality marked by reduced consumer confidence and stringent market dynamics. This environment demanded innovative approaches to business strategies that not only focused on survival but also aimed for growth. A common strategy was pivoting to digital transformation, which involved the rapid adoption of e-commerce platforms and social media marketing to reach a broader audience. Local artisans, once limited to physical markets, began crafting online stores, enabling them to sell directly to consumers. This shift illustrates the power of adaptability; companies that embraced technology not only weathered the storm but also expanded their market reach. Entrepreneurs commonly reported that this transition fueled customer engagement and loyalty, reinforcing the critical lesson that innovation can act as a lifeline. Moving forward, businesses are encouraged to assess their operational models and explore how digital tools can enhance efficiency and connectivity, inviting readers to reflect on their own business practices. In addition to embracing technology, many firms recognized the importance of fostering resilience through agile business practices. Instead of rigid structures, companies adopted flexible strategies that allowed them to react swiftly to changing consumer preferences and market conditions. A small organic farm, for example, shifted from wholesale distribution to a community-supported agriculture model, enabling them to connect more deeply with their customer base. This novel approach not only secured a steady income stream during uncertain times but also cultivated a loyal community around their cause. Thus, businesses that emphasized adaptability began to view crisis not merely as a threat but as an opportunity for reinvention. A practical exercise remains for entrepreneurs and managers alike: consider a recent operational challenge and outline three innovative strategies to address it. This reflection is a crucial step in building a more resilient future.

A critical component of innovative business strategies post-crisis is the emphasis on sustainable practices. Companies that incorporate environmental and social governance into their business models not only attract conscious consumers but also create long-term value. The data is compelling: firms that adopt sustainable practices tend to outperform their peers financially, benefiting from lower operational costs and enhanced brand loyalty. Consider a tech startup that integrated eco-friendly materials into their products while simultaneously prioritizing employee well-being. Such practices exemplify the principle of purpose-driven business, which resonates deeply with the modern consumer. As businesses contemplate their roles in a post-crisis economy, they must also assess how aligned their missions are with societal values. A reflection for readers could entail identifying ways their products or services could innovate for sustainability, fostering not just economic freedom but also contributing positively to the world around them.

LESSONS LEARNED FROM ENTREPRENEURIAL SUCCESS

Navigating the uncertain waters of the entrepreneurial landscape often mirrors a rollercoaster ride, filled with unexpected highs and cavernous lows. Families who have witnessed financial hardships frequently rally around stories of resilience, learning to adapt and thrive when facing challenges. Success in entrepreneurship often hinges on a crucial lesson: the importance of a finely tuned financial literacy. This involves not only understanding the intricacies of personal finance but also recognizing how economic factors —like inflation rates and interest levels—impact ones enterprise. A common thread among successful entrepreneurs is their ability to translate hard data into actionable steps, guiding them through setbacks and ultimately leading them to sustainable growth. One entrepreneur might recall the painful missteps taken during the last recession, from miscalculating cash flow to underestimating the importance of a financial cushion. These lessons shape their approach today, making them more vigilant and proactive in their fiscal strategies.

The art of reinvesting wisely stands out as a vital strategy practiced by those who have succeeded in the entrepreneurial realm. Entrepreneurs who consistently prioritize reinvestment not merely in financial terms but also through continuous education and employee development tend to enjoy long-term sustainability. One family, having faced bankruptcy during the economic downturn, transformed their business model by incorporating lessons learned from their past mistakes. They instituted a practice of regularly revisiting their investment strategies and tracking performance metrics in real-time. This adaptability not only allowed them to weather current challenges but also positioned them for growth when the economy started to stabilize. Reflecting on their journey, they stress the importance of having a mentorship system or community for support, highlighting how shared experiences can lead to deeper insights that might otherwise go unnoticed.

Creating a solid safety net is a non-negotiable lesson that emerges from exploring entrepreneurial success stories. The unpredictability of markets and shifting consumer behaviors makes it essential for entrepreneurs to have a robust contingency plan. Anecdotes of individuals who revived their businesses after unexpected hurdles often center around the sacrifices made to establish this safety net: funneling personal savings into an emergency fund or scaling back on personal expenditures to increase business liquidity. One inspiring story comes from a small business owner who, after navigating through tumultuous economic tides, made it a priority to allocate a percentage of earnings into a reserve fund each month. This proactive approach provided her with peace of mind and flexibility to pivot when necessary, reinforcing her commitment to economic independence. Readers are encouraged to assess their financial reserves and tailor their saving strategies to align with both personal goals and unforeseen challenges, thereby solidifying their own safety net for the future.

XII. THE PSYCHOLOGY OF MONEY

Everyday financial decisions can feel overwhelming, especially in the wake of an economic crisis that has left many reeling. When faced with uncertainty, it's common for individuals to revert to ingrained psychological behaviors about money, often prioritizing immediate gratification over long-term financial well-being. This notion is starkly illustrated by the experiences of families who previously lived paycheck to paycheck. One such family, the Garcias, found themselves trapped in a cycle of high-interest debt, struggling to make ends meet. Conversations with their financial advisor revealed a disheartening trend: a reluctance to confront their financial fears often led to poor choices. The psychological implications of such decisions manifest in anxiety and disempowerment, underscoring the need for a comprehensive understanding of how emotions shape financial behavior. By recognizing these patterns, readers can begin to challenge their own beliefs and embrace a more proactive stance toward financial planning.

In exploring the psychological facets of money management, it becomes critical to recognize the role of education—or its glaring absence. Many individuals enter adulthood without the necessary tools to navigate complex financial landscapes, a gap illuminated by the 2008 financial crisis. Young adults emerging from college found themselves burdened by student loans, compounded by a lack of knowledge in managing their finances. Interviews with recent graduates reveal a shared sentiment of confusion, particularly regarding budgeting and saving. This financial illiteracy exacerbates a culture of dependence on credit, leading to further economic pitfalls. Equipping individuals with foundational financial education not only promotes responsible spending but also empowers them to break free from cyclical debt. Thus, transforming financial habits begins with addressing the systemic issues in education systems that neglect life skills in favor of traditional academic curricula.

The "RICH Method 2.0" advocates for a shift from mere survival to proactive engagement with money, emphasizing purpose-driven financial behavior. This approach begins with a proactive assessment of income and expenses, urging individuals to reinvest in their growth. Stories of families who implemented these principles illustrate the potential for a substantial turnaround. The Rodriguez family, for instance, established a safety net by reallocating unused subscription expenses towards savings, successfully creating a buffer against future uncertainties. By harnessing a supportive network, they cultivated a community of accountability, whereby financial goals were regularly evaluated and revised. As illustrated through personal anecdotes, these steps toward financial discipline not only promote economic stability but also foster a sense of agency. The concluding exercises of this section encourage readers to evaluate their own financial habits, setting forth on a path toward achieving long-term freedom and security in an increasingly volatile economic landscape.

MINDSET SHIFTS FOR FINANCIAL SUCCESS

As individuals navigate the financial landscape shaped by past recessions, the importance of a proactive mindset becomes undeniably clear. Picture a recent college graduate, fresh out of school, burdened with student loans yet passionate about starting a small business. By instead of succumbing to her fears of debt, she begins viewing her financial situation as a canvas for growth and opportunity. This shift in perception is vital; it transforms a daunting debt load into a manageable stepping stone towards financial independence. Empirical research underscores this connection between mindset and financial behavior, revealing that those who see their financial challenges as surmountable tend to adopt healthier financial habits. This mindset, bolstered by an attitude of learning, encourages practical strategies like budgeting and smart investing. Individuals who cultivate resilience in their financial thinking not only prepare for unforeseen challenges but also build the necessary confidence to pursue their economic ambitions.

Consider the case of a family that experienced significant financial strain during an economic downturn. Initially, they viewed their situation through a lens of scarcity, focusing on immediate survival rather than long-term planning. After attending a financial workshop that emphasized the importance of mindset over mere knowledge, they began to strategize differently. They learned the power of improving expense efficiency, leading them to reevaluate their budget and seek new sources of income. This revelation is not just anecdotal; it is supported by data indicating that families adopting these practices often see a marked improvement in their savings rates. Their transformation underscores a fundamental lesson: successful financial management requires more than mere numbers—it demands a shift from a scarcity mindset to one that embraces abundance and possibility. In redefining their relationship with money, they not only improved their finances but also fostered a nurturing environment for their children, reinforcing positive financial habits for future generations.

Mindset shifts are not solely about individual perspectives; they collectively influence broader economic behavior in significant ways. When communities adopt a mindset of empowerment, the ripple effect can stimulate local economies, evidenced by entrepreneurial initiatives springing up post-recession. Take a small neighborhood where multiple residents, inspired by shared success stories, band together to form an investment cooperative. What began as a few cautious discussions turned into a collaborative approach to reinvesting wisely, further enhancing the community's financial resilience. This evolution illustrates how collective mindset shifts can galvanize a culture of economic freedom, drawing on the strengths of diverse community members. Each individual's learning curve contributes to a broader fabric of financial literacy, emphasizing the importance of harnessing purpose driven saving as a communal goal. As readers reflect on their personal financial journeys, they are encouraged to seek opportunities for collaboration, creating potential microeconomies that foster independence and growth. Consider setting a goal to connect with someone in your community to share financial insights, thereby cultivating both personal and collective wealth.

EMOTIONAL RELATIONSHIP WITH MONEY

In the wake of financial crises, many individuals experience a tumultuous emotional relationship with money that impacts their decision-making and overall financial health. Consider the story of a middle-class family in Spain, who, after losing their home due to excessive mortgage debt, grappled with feelings of shame and anxiety over their financial situation. Their narrative reveals a pervasive cycle of stress that often accompanies economic instability, characterized by irrational spending and a fear of budgeting. This emotional turbulence is backed by recent studies indicating that psychological factors significantly influence financial behaviors. In this light, understanding and unraveling the complex emotional ties to money can empower individuals to break free from detrimental cycles. The challenge lies in reframing these emotions, transforming anxiety into motivation for better financial habits—a crucial initial step in the RICH Method 2.0 approach. Transitioning from fear to empowerment requires practical tools and relatable strategies that address emotional triggers associated with money. Recognizing that many people conflate self-worth with net worth can illuminate this transformation. A successful entrepreneur once shared how detaching her identity from her bank balance enabled her to take calculated risks, which ultimately led to financial success. By fostering a mindset centered on personal growth and resilience, individuals can confront their financial fears instead of allowing them to dictate their choices. Incorporating techniques such as mindful budgeting or gratitude journaling provides individuals with concrete strategies to reshape their emotional relationship with money. These practices not only promote a more positive outlook towards ones financial situation but also lay the groundwork for sustainable financial literacy—a core component of the RICH Method 2.0. The conclusion to this emotional journey with money comes not just from understanding and reframing feelings but also from actionable commitments to change. Engaging in exercises that promote financial literacy, such as setting up a clear spending plan, helps ground individuals in their newfound financial awareness. Consider the simple act of tracking daily expenses: it can illuminate spending patterns while simultaneously evoking a sense of ownership and control. By implementing small yet impactful changes, individuals can combat longstanding anxieties and foster a more constructive financial mindset. The RICH Method 2.0 encourages such practices as stepping stones towards achieving economic freedom. As readers embark on their financial journeys, they are invited to view money not as a source of stress but as a tool for empowerment—a shift that could ultimately lead to a more harmonious relationship with their finances.

STRATEGIES TO OVERCOME FINANCIAL ANXIETY

Imagine standing in line at the grocery store, feeling the weight of every item in your cart as the cashier rings them up. Anxiety swells in your stomach; the prices keep climbing, and questions about your budget flood your mind. This scenario is all too common for those grappling with financial stress. One effective strategy for overcoming financial anxiety involves establishing a transparent budgeting process. By creating a detailed budget that categorizes fixed and variable expenses, individuals can better visualize their cash flow. Tracking expenditures through user-friendly apps or even simple spreadsheets makes the task less daunting. Behavioral insights reveal that spending awareness often leads to more conscious purchasing decisions. This practice not only alleviates the cognitive load associated with money management but also fosters a sense of empowerment. As you assess your spending habits, consider committing to a weekly review session, where you can recalibrate and make informed choices about your financial future.

In the face of financial uncertainty, many people feel trapped by existing obligations and debt. Yet, restructuring personal debt represents another powerful strategy to reclaim control over ones finances and reduce anxiety. With rising interest rates, individuals often overlook the benefits of negotiating payment terms or consolidating loans. By proactively reaching out to creditors and exploring options such as lower interest rates or extended payment plans, one can effectively ease financial pressures. Personal stories reveal that those who took the initiative to manage their debts reported significant psychological relief, finding renewed hope for their financial futures. Resources, including nonprofit credit counseling, can provide guidance on effective negotiation techniques and realistic repayment strategies. Practical exercises, such as listing out all debts alongside interest rates and payment terms, can illuminate potential areas for improvement, allowing individuals to create actionable plans tailored to their unique circumstances. Beyond immediate financial strategies, developing a robust emergency fund can play a crucial role in mitigating anxiety. The popular saying expect the unexpected resonates profoundly in the context of personal finance. Economic downturns can occur with little warning, underscoring the importance of creating a financial buffer. Studies indicate that maintaining three to six months' worth of living expenses in a readily accessible account significantly enhances financial security and reduces stress. By setting aside a small percentage of income regularly, individuals can shift their mindset from one of survival to one of stability and preparedness. Real-life testimonials often highlight how families experienced a profound sense of relief once they built their safety nets, enabling them to tackle unexpected expenses confidently. To begin this journey, consider setting a monthly savings goal and automating transfers into a high-yield savings account, transforming the daunting task of saving into an achievable habit.

XIII. THE IMPORTANCE OF COMMUNITY SUPPORT

In the aftermath of financial crises, it is often communities that rally together, offering both tangible and intangible support to those hardest hit. Consider the scenario of a neighborhood facing a local business closure—what ensues is not merely despair but a surge of solidarity. Residents may organize fundraisers, volunteer days, or collective buying initiatives to ensure the business's survival and maintain local economic vibrancy. These small-scale actions not only help to sustain the business but also bolster community ties, reinforcing the idea that economic resilience often hinges on social interconnectedness. Data indicates that communities with strong social networks tend to bounce back more quickly from economic downturns. The ethos of community support serves as a reminder that the journey toward financial independence is seldom walked alone, reinforcing the interconnectedness between personal finance and collective welfare. The importance of community support becomes evident through shared resources and knowledge, an essential aspect of financial literacy. People often overlook that valuable financial education is available not just in books or online courses, but within their own communities. Picture a pair of neighbors exchanging budgeting tips or a local workshop led by a retired accountant sharing real-world insights. These informal interactions can demystify personal finance concepts, ultimately empowering individuals to make informed decisions. The shared experiences, particularly those involving hardships and successes during financial struggles, create a rich tapestry of practical lessons. By embracing local knowledge-sharing traditions, individuals can foster an environment where financial advice is accessible and relatable, enhancing each members ability to navigate economic challenges. This community-driven initiative transforms financial education from a solitary task into a collaborative venture, strengthening ties in the process. The emotional aspect of financial support within a community cannot be overstated. During times of economic hardship, the psychological weight of financial stress can lead to isolation and anxiety. When neighbors come together to share their burdens, remarkable transformations can occur. Consider the story of a small local group that formed during a recent economic downturn, dedicating themselves to bi-weekly discussions about savings and investments. These meetings not only provided valuable insights but also a safe space for members to express their fears and ambitions regarding their finances. The emotional support acts as a buffer against the negative effects of financial distress, fostering resilience and motivation. This notion of emotional backing complements the technical aspects of finance, highlighting that true economic freedom is not just about numbers but about the strength built within community connections. To harness this, individuals can initiate or participate in local financial discussion groups, transforming personal finance into a communal journey.

BUILDING A SUPPORT NETWORK

Navigating the financial landscape can often feel isolating, yet building a robust support network is a pivotal strategy for attaining personal financial stability. Consider the story of Maria, a single mother living in a modest apartment who struggled to balance bills and childcare. During a community workshop, she discovered the importance of connecting with local resources and like-minded individuals facing similar financial hurdles. Maria found that by sharing her challenges, she could receive not only emotional support but also practical advice tailored to her circumstance. By pooling resources and knowledge within her network, she became empowered to make informed decisions and ultimately transformed her financial management. Such personal anecdotes reflect broader trends indicating that individuals who actively cultivate supportive relationships tend to navigate financial crises more effectively. As you reflect on your experiences, think about the people around you: what role could they play in your financial journey? Establishing a support network requires more than just attendance at social events; it involves intentionality and commitment to cultivating relationships that offer reciprocal benefits. Seeking out local financial literacy workshops or joining online forums can create connections that extend beyond mere acquaintances. Data shows that individuals who engage with financial communities learn about budgeting techniques, investment opportunities, and risk management strategies faster than those who try to go it alone. By prioritizing active participation, individuals can more readily share experiences, challenges, and successes, fostering a culture of collective resilience. Envision attending regular meet-ups where diverse voices discuss and demystify financial topics, much like a book club for personal finance. By the end of each interaction, members leave not only with new insights but also with a renewed sense of accountability.

Consider forming or joining such a group; envision the possibilities when collaboration becomes the norm.

The essence of a support network lies in its diversity, encompassing individuals from varying financial backgrounds and experiences. Each voice adds a unique perspective, enriching the decision-making process and sparking innovative solutions to shared challenges. A retiree with years of financial wisdom can offer insights into long-term planning that resonate with younger members facing immediate concerns. Such intergenerational dialogue can foster skills that many may find lacking, such as understanding market trends or developing a nuanced approach to risk. The empowering narrative generated by these exchanges can dismantle the stigma associated with financial struggles, turning vulnerability into a source of strength. Actively seek to expand your network to include diverse voices and experiences. As your next practical exercise, identify at least three people who can contribute unique perspectives to your financial journey, and arrange a meeting to discuss your financial goals and hurdles.

SHARING RESOURCES AND KNOWLEDGE

In the wake of the recent economic crisis, many individuals found themselves grappling not just with personal financial dilemmas, but with a collective sense of disconnection from reliable sources of financial wisdom. The shared experiences of families navigating these turbulent waters illuminate the importance of resource-sharing and knowledge exchange. A single mother in Madrid discovered that by joining a local financial literacy group, she could access advice that was previously out of reach. Each session featured members sharing their successes and setbacks, fostering an environment where practical tips—like budgeting strategies and saving hacks—could be discussed openly. This communal spirit not only alleviated individual burdens but also enhanced collective financial acumen, prompting an emergent renaissance of economic literacy rooted in personal narratives and practical experience.

The integration of hard data into discussions of financial education plain illustrates the urgency for reform in our approach to knowledge sharing. Studies show that households engaging in community-driven financial workshops report higher savings rates and reduced stress associated with debt. This phenomenon can be attributed to the power of peer support and shared accountability; when individuals see others taking tangible steps toward financial stability, it inspires a sense of urgency and motivation that statistics alone cannot evoke. Consider, for instance, a small cohort of entrepreneurs in Valencia who began trading advice and resources, resulting in an uptick in their individual business revenues. It was not merely the financial tips they exchanged, but the encouragement derived from their shared journeys that propelled them forward. This kind of resource-sharing emerges as a core tenet of the RICH Method 2.0, emphasizing economic empowerment through collaboration.

Navigating the complexities of personal finance can feel isolating, yet the process itself often becomes more manageable when approached in a community setting. Individuals frequently express feelings of vulnerability when discussing their financial situations; sharing knowledge turns this vulnerability into collective strength. A father in Barcelona recounted how weekly meetings with fellow parents not only helped him understand investments better but also encouraged him to actively participate in family budgeting discussions. This shift didn't merely improve his financial literacy; it rekindled deeper family conversations about goals and priorities, thereby fostering a culture of financial transparency at home. To harness this power of shared knowledge effectively, it is essential to engage in community-based exercises, such as initiating a resource-sharing group or finding a financial accountability partner. Embracing these practices could significantly enhance ones path toward economic freedom while nurturing a supportive network of informed individuals.

CASE STUDIES OF COMMUNITY-BASED FINANCIAL SUCCESS

Every community has at least one story that exemplifies the power of collective economic action. In a small town in Spain, a group of local entrepreneurs faced a challenging economic climate following the last recession. They banded together to establish a cooperative that not only revitalized their businesses but also fortified their local economy. By sharing resources, from marketing strategies to financial literacy workshops, these entrepreneurs cultivated a supportive environment where knowledge and financial acumen flourished. This grassroots initiative not only led to an increase in individual profit margins, but it also fostered a communal sense of ownership and responsibility among members. Such success stories illustrate the efficacy of community-based financial strategies: when individuals pool their resources and insights, they create a formidable network that can weather economic downturns. For readers eager to embark on a similar journey, consider organizing or joining local networks that emphasize shared financial education and cooperative investments as a first step towards economic improvement. As communities pivot towards resilience, the integration of technology has proven instrumental in facilitating financial success. Take, for instance, the innovative use of mobile financial applications in underserved neighborhoods that were previously trapped in cycles of predatory lending. By providing users access to budgeting tools and educational resources directly through their smartphones, these apps have empowered residents to make informed financial decisions. During a recent interview with a local financial advisor, the advisor highlighted a case where a single mother utilized these tools to not only escape credit card debt but also to establish an emergency savings fund. Her story resonates with many individuals grappling with financial instability, showcasing how technology can demystify personal finance and serve as a catalyst for change. This raises the question: how can community members leverage available technology to build their financial knowledge? Readers can start by exploring budgeting apps and participating in online financial literacy webinars tailored to their unique circumstances. The intersection of personal finance and community support can lead to transformative outcomes, as evidenced by the triumphs of local microfinance initiatives. In various urban centers, community-based lending programs have empowered residents to launch their own businesses, breaking free from traditional credit constraints. Through these initiatives, local banks and non-profits offer small loans accompanied by financial guidance and mentorship, fostering entrepreneurship in neighborhoods historically overlooked by conventional financial institutions. One participants journey illustrates this point; after receiving a modest loan, she was able to open a small bakery, creating job opportunities for others in her community. This ripple effect illustrates how microfinance not only addresses immediate funding needs but also nurtures local economies. To capitalize on such opportunities, readers should investigate local microfinance programs or cooperatives that could support their aspirations. Consider how the power of community-focused financial solutions can play a crucial role in achieving economic freedom and resilience in the face of future challenges.

XIV. TECHNOLOGY IN PERSONAL FINANCE

In today's fast-paced environment, individuals often find themselves overwhelmed by the myriad of financial decisions that lie ahead. Imagine Sarah, a young professional, anxiously glancing at her overdraft balance and endless credit card statements. Faced with such turmoil, a strategic embrace of technology can fundamentally reshape her financial narrative and offer a glimmer of hope. The emergence of personal finance apps and budgeting tools allows users to streamline their financial habits and gain unparalleled insights into their spending patterns. By harnessing data analytics, these platforms help demystify complex financial information, enabling users to make informed decisions swiftly. This transformative potential lies not just in automation but in fostering accountability, as users receive timely reminders and alerts tailored to their financial goals. As Sarah, in our scenario, implements these solutions, she discovers the power of technology as an ally rather than a hindrance in her quest for economic stability.

Yet, while technology provides indispensable resources, it cannot replace the personal dimension of financial management. Take, for instance, the experience of John, a family man who relied on a newly adopted finance tracking app. Initially, he felt isolated in his efforts, believing he alone was responsible for overcoming the financial pitfalls he faced. Dynamic communities within these platforms now offer shared advice and personal stories from users who have trodden similar paths. This interplay of shared experiences and technological innovation creates an environment ripe for growth. By encouraging interactions among users, financial apps act as catalysts, transforming mundane budgeting into a communal journey towards shared goals. Johns story reflects the profound ethos of the RICH Method 2.0, highlighting that the power of technology manifests not solely through data but also through supportive networks that empower individuals in their economic pursuits.

The adoption of technology in personal finance serves not only to facilitate better financial oversight but also to cultivate a forward-thinking mindset. Visualize a household engaged in an initiative where they set collective savings goals, leveraging digital tools to track progress collaboratively. By examining trends in their financial behavior, families can halt cyclical patterns of debt and instead, orient their resources towards value driven objectives. This proactive engagement transforms passive consumption into strategic investments in experiences and wealth-building endeavors. The challenge presented by the RICH Method 2.0 becomes clear: it encourages individuals to adopt a hands-on approach with the aids of technology, inspiring them to take charge of their future. As families commit to this journey, they can turn their data into actionable insights, paving pathways towards economic freedom and resilience in times of uncertainty.

TOOLS FOR BUDGETING AND TRACKING

Imagine a young couple, Maria and Javier, who found themselves overwhelmed by debt after losing their jobs during the economic crisis. In their quest for financial stability, they learned to use budgeting tools not just as a means to track expenses but as a pathway to empowerment. Digital budgeting apps such as Mint and YNAB (You Need A Budget) emerged as essential allies for them, providing user-friendly interfaces that helped them categorize spending, set financial goals, and visualize their progress. The emotional weight that lifted as they systematically planned their months, even amid uncertainty, was transformative; these apps turned a daunting task into an engaging experience. Their story illustrates how integrating technology into personal finance can lead to newfound clarity and control. As a practical exercise, readers are encouraged to explore various budgeting tools and select one that resonates with their financial goals, setting a clear intention to utilize it daily for a month. As Maria and Javier embraced their budgeting app, they began to analyze their spending patterns, unveiling the stark reality of their financial habits. It became evident that unwittingly overspending on dining out and entertainment was hindering their ability to save. By leveraging the analytical features of their chosen app, they discovered not just where to cut back but how to reallocate those funds toward building an emergency fund. This focus on data-driven decisions marked a shift in their relationship with money — from being passive participants to proactive managers of their finances. Their experience underscores the critical role that detailed expense tracking plays in personal finance. For readers, a reflective exercise is posed: keep a weekly diary of expenditures for one month to better understand where their money flows and identify opportunities for improvement in their budgeting habits.

Understanding that mere budgeting is not a panacea, Maria and Javier sought tools with a holistic approach to financial tracking. They integrated income tracking services that allowed them to account for fluctuating income, a common reality in a gig economy. This step empowered them to create more accurate forecasts and adjust their budgets accordingly, demonstrating the necessity of flexibility in financial planning. They engaged with financial literacy resources such as webinars and online courses, which fostered a deeper comprehension of investments and savings. Their evolving story accentuates the importance of combining various financial tools, acknowledging that effective budgeting encompasses monitoring not only spending but also overall wealth growth. Readers are urged to consider diversifying their financial toolkit by attending a financial literacy seminar or exploring an online course, reinforcing the notion that continuous education is integral to achieving long-term economic freedom.

IMPACT OF FINTECH ON PERSONAL FINANCE

Navigating the financial landscape can often feel overwhelming, especially in the wake of a crisis. Imagine a family grappling with student loans, struggling to save while balancing everyday expenses like groceries and childcare. For many, traditional banking services have become burdensome, laden with fees and complicated procedures. Enter fintech, which has revolutionized personal finance by democratizing access to financial tools. Applications for budgeting, investing, and debt management appear at our fingertips, simplifying previously daunting tasks. Recent studies reveal that over 70% of consumers who use fintech tools have reported improved savings rates, demonstrating a tangible shift toward financial health. This technological advancement not only helps individuals regain control over their finances but also fosters a greater understanding of money management principles. The ease of use and accessibility provided by fintech can empower people to tackle their own financial challenges with confidence and clarity, suggesting that technology may serve as a crucial ally in the quest for economic freedom. Supplementing traditional banks, fintech offers innovative solutions that cater to a wide variety of financial needs, making it essential for individuals to leverage these advancements. Think of Maria, a single mother who previously relied on high-interest payday loans, a trend that often traps borrowers in cycles of debt. By utilizing crowdfunding platforms and peer-to-peer lending options, she has not only accessed lower interest rates but has also developed a supportive community that encourages financial literacy. Data from the OECD indicates that countries embracing fintech have experienced faster economic recovery post-crisis, underscoring its potential as a financial lifeline for many. As families like Marias begin to harness these tools, they pave the way for improved fiscal accountability and entrepreneurship, ultimately contributing to a more robust economy. This transition highlights the necessity for personal finance education, where understanding fintech becomes paramount to achieving long-term financial stability and success. Having integrated fintech into personal finance strategies, the need for proactive financial literacy emerges as essential for navigating this new terrain successfully. Envision a group discussion among friends who are sharing their experiences with different apps that help track expenses or compare savings rates. Within these dialogues lies the potential to empower individuals with knowledge that can significantly enhance their financial literacy. Many fintech applications now include educational components that simplify complex financial concepts, bridging the gap left by traditional education systems. In encouraging the adoption of the RICH method, it is essential that users not only utilize these technologies but also engage with them critically, adapting their newfound knowledge to their unique situations. Consequently, individuals should establish weekly check-ins, perhaps using a shared digital planner, to review financial goals and track their progress. Such practical exercises encourage accountability and community support, solidifying the foundation for long-term economic freedom.

FUTURE TRENDS IN FINANCIAL TECHNOLOGY

Financial technology is not merely evolving; its rapidly transforming the very landscape of personal finance, driven by both innovation and necessity. As households grapple with the aftereffects of economic uncertainty, the growing accessibility of digital financial tools presents new pathways for empowerment. Technologies such as artificial intelligence and machine learning are reshaping how individuals interact with their finances, enabling personalized budgeting systems that adapt to spending habits in real time. These advancements allow family financial planners to create tailored advice that resonates with users' unique situations, illustrating how financial management can become more intuitive. A relatable story emerges from a single mother who, after downloading a budgeting app, not only managed to track her expenses but also stumbled upon investment opportunities she never considered. By leveraging these resources, individuals can transform their financial literacy and cultivate a more profound sense of economic freedom, paving the way for sound decision-making.

As we look ahead, the impending shift towards decentralized finance (DeFi) is set to redefine traditional banking methods, challenging the status quo. Centralized institutions have long been the gatekeepers of financial opportunities, but DeFi promises to democratize access, allowing users to lend, borrow, and trade without intermediaries. This paradigm shift can be particularly significant for underserved communities historically locked out of conventional banking systems. Imagine a local entrepreneur able to secure a microloan through blockchain technology rather than enduring the paperwork and delays of a traditional bank. Such scenarios exemplify the potential for economic liberation in the hands of individuals, inviting more people to engage in financial activities that facilitate growth. Yet, this innovation also demands a cautious approach to education; individuals must understand the risks inherent in these new models. Integrating practical exercises that encourage participants to explore these innovations safely is essential for instilling confidence. Emerging trends in sustainability-linked finance are reshaping investment priorities and encouraging a more responsible management of resources. As environmental issues become central to public discourse, the financial sector is responding with products aimed at promoting sustainability. Eco-conscious investment vehicles, such as green bonds and sustainability-focused funds, are not only appealing to socially responsible investors but are also edging into the mainstream. This movement toward ethical investing is inspiring a new generation of savers, eager to align their financial goals with their values. A poignant example can be found in a family deciding to invest their savings in a local renewable energy initiative, thereby supporting both their community and their financial future. Encouraging readers to consider these options not only promotes responsible financial behavior but also emphasizes the role that individual choices play in the larger scheme of economic stability. Engaging in investment strategies that prioritize sustainability is presented as both a personal and collective exercise, inviting readers to step into a financially responsible future that also contributes to broader societal prosperity.

XV. CULTURAL ATTITUDES TOWARD MONEY

Amid the turbulence of the economic crisis, cultural attitudes toward money significantly shaped individual behaviors and societal norms. Many people, faced with uncertainty, gravitated toward frugality and cautious spending habits, redefining what financial security truly means. In interviews with families affected by job loss, one compelling story often emerged: the shift from viewing money as a transactional tool to understanding it as a means to navigate life's uncertainties. Maria, a single mother from Madrid, recounts how she learned to budget with an eye toward preserving her family's quality of life rather than simply chasing after material possessions. This shift, seen in various demographics during the recovery, reveals a broader theme: the elevation of experience and resilience over consumption. Viewing money through a pragmatic lens fosters a necessary dialogue about economic choices and the long-term benefits of financial discipline. As societies grapple with their relationship to wealth, common themes are evident in diverse cultural attitudes. For some communities, money is synonymous with hope and opportunity; for others, it becomes a source of anxiety and inequality. Statistical data show pronounced disparities in saving behaviors across different socioeconomic groups, which tie back to cultural beliefs about money. In interviews with financial advisors, it becomes clear that those who grow up in households where money discussions were open tend to embrace financial literacy more readily. In contrast, families marked by financial struggle often perpetuate cycles of ignorance around money management. These contrasting narratives underscore the need for more inclusive financial education that respects various cultural backgrounds, enabling individuals to break free from limiting perceptions and foster a healthier relationship with their finances.

Transforming cultural attitudes toward money is not merely an academic exercise; it has concrete implications for economic freedom. This evolution often necessitates community-driven initiatives, where users actively engage in workshops and discussions that challenge prevailing financial myths. The "RICH Method 2.0" serves as an outline for such transformative experiences, encouraging participants to take actionable steps based on their newly discovered attitudes. After a community workshop, attendees often report taking deliberate steps toward creating emergency funds or engaging in investment groups. Such collective empowerment reinforces the importance of shared experiences in shaping personal finance strategies. Closing each chapter with practical exercises reinforces these ideas, inviting readers to reflect on their financial beliefs and explore innovative solutions for their economic futures. Through this synthesis of cultural understanding and practical steps, individuals can reclaim their financial destiny and inspire others on a similar journey toward stability and abundance.

HOW CULTURE INFLUENCES FINANCIAL DECISIONS

In an era marked by economic uncertainty, the cultural frameworks within which individuals operate play a pivotal role in shaping their financial behaviors and decisions. In a recent conversation with Maria, a single mother in a small Spanish town, she shared that her upbringing emphasized saving and avoiding debt. This background informed her approach to managing her finances; Maria is reticent about using credit cards, a common practice among her peers. Instead, she prioritizes saving for her children's education, illustrating how cultural values around money can dictate personal finance strategies. Integral to the discourse on financial decision-making is the acknowledgment that these culturally embedded beliefs often arise from historical contexts, including economic hardships faced by previous generations. As such, understanding one's cultural orientation towards money management enables an examination of both conscious and unconscious influences at play, which can lead to impactful financial outcomes.

The intersection of social norms with financial decision-making manifests not only at the individual level but also within broader communities, highlighting how cultural narratives can dictate collective attitudes toward wealth. In a neighborhood where conspicuous consumption is celebrated, many families might feel pressured to maintain appearances through luxury purchases, despite underlying debt. This notion was echoed in interviews with local financial advisors who noted that clients often struggle with balancing cultural expectations against their financial realities. Such situations underscore the psychological weight of cultural influences; individuals may adhere to societal pressures that fundamentally undermine their financial health. The collective behavior of communities can perpetuate cycles of financial instability or stability, depending on whether these narratives support prudent fiscal management or encourage reckless spending. Understanding these dynamics is essential for any financial improvement strategy aiming to foster economic freedom. To mitigate the adverse effects of cultural influences on financial decisions, awareness and education serve as powerful tools for transformation. Engaging with various perspectives on money—whether through workshops, community discussions, or personal finance literature—can help reshape one's financial narrative. A practical exercise for readers might involve reflecting on their own cultural upbringing regarding money. By identifying key influences—such as family beliefs, societal norms, and personal experiences—individuals can better understand how these elements steer their financial decisions. This self-awareness is the first step toward cultivating healthier financial habits that align with ones values rather than being dictated solely by cultural expectations. Fostering a critical perspective on culture's role in finance can empower individuals to reclaim their economic future, moving from reactive responses to deliberate financial choices that lead toward economic freedom.

COMPARATIVE ANALYSIS OF SPANISH AND GLOBAL ATTITUDES

In the aftermath of the 2008 financial crisis, Spain's economic landscape was marred by skyrocketing unemployment rates and stagnant wages, reflecting a unique blend of collective trauma and resilience. Families in Spain often found themselves grappling with spiraling debt, as mortgage levels became unsustainable for many, a stark contrast to global trends where some countries recovered relatively swiftly. Personal anecdotes, such as the story of a working-class family in Madrid struggling to keep their home, underscore the stark realities of financial insecurity. This intensified sense of urgency catalyzed a reevaluation of financial practices, pushing individuals to reassess their saving strategies and spending habits. Global comparisons reveal that while Spanish households faced exceptional challenges, they also exhibited a remarkable adaptability through community support and local initiatives. This disparity emphasizes not only the unique cultural responses to economic crises but also highlights the shared need for enhanced financial education and proactive planning in the face of economic vulnerability.

Spanish attitudes toward personal finance have evolved significantly, often characterized by a cautious approach influenced by recent economic experiences. In contrast to more risk-tolerant global counterparts, many Spaniards approach investments with trepidation, preferring to save in traditional forms rather than venture into potentially lucrative but unfamiliar financial instruments. Interviews with younger Spanish professionals reveal a prevalent sentiment: despite growing awareness of diverse investment opportunities, the specter of past financial failures looms large, shaping a generally conservative outlook. This hesitation impacts broader economic trends, as Spain lags behind nations that embrace innovative financial solutions and entrepreneurial ventures. Addressing these attitudes is essential for advancing economic freedom in Spain, suggesting that a paradigm shift in how financial risks are perceived could lead to improved stability and growth. Engaging with financial advisors who emphasize informed risk-taking may empower individuals to diversify their portfolios, ultimately enhancing long-term economic resilience.

In analyzing the comparative attitudes toward financial freedom, it becomes evident that bridging the gap between Spanish caution and global innovation requires a concerted effort towards education and practical engagement. The RICH Method 2.0, with its four pillars, offers a adaptable framework for individuals and families looking to reclaim their financial independence, particularly in a Spanish context where traditional savings mechanisms dominate. By instilling a culture of reinvestment and purposeful saving, the method encourages a shift from mere survival to proactive financial health. An everyday scenario might involve a family leveraging newly acquired budgeting skills to pay down debts while simultaneously setting aside funds for investment opportunities. This not only cultivates economic freedom but also fosters a community oriented mindset, emphasizing collective growth. The call to action here is straightforward: by stepping outside their comfort zones and exploring avenues for informed financial decision-making, Spaniards can enhance their economic futures, embracing a broader global financial perspective and reaping its benefits.

Indicator	Spain	Global Average
Economic Freedom Index Score	69.9	60
Business Freedom Index Score	7.44	6.5
Financial Freedom Index Score	70	65
Household Saving Rate (% of gross disposable income)	7.9	10
Unemployment Rate	12.14	5

Comparative Analysis of Spanish and Global Attitudes Towards Personal Finance and Economic Freedom

STRATEGIES TO SHIFT CULTURAL PERCEPTIONS

The echoes of the financial crisis serve as a powerful reminder of the consequences stemming from unaddressed behavioral patterns surrounding money. Personal anecdotes of families who faced significant economic upheaval illustrate the critical need for a seamless shift in cultural perceptions related to financial literacy and responsibility. One family discussed how, prior to implementing the RICH Method 2.0, they operated under the belief that financial success was solely dependent on high income. After experiencing a severe downturn, they realized that managing expenses and understanding debt played a pivotal role in their financial wellbeing. This shift in mindset not only led them to embrace budgeting but also fueled their determination to educate their children about finances from an early age. As such, fostering a new cultural narrative around money management can catalyze positive change at both individual and community levels, encouraging discussions that promote financial responsibility. Transitioning cultural perceptions necessitates engaging with youth, who often carry the brunt of financial ignorance into adulthood. The implementation of comprehensive financial education programs in schools is one viable strategy to reshape attitudes toward saving and spending. When youth learn about concepts like interest rates, investment strategies, and effective budgeting early on, they develop healthier financial habits that often persist throughout their lives. One school program successfully incorporated experiential learning by having students manage a small budget for a mock event, allowing them to see firsthand the consequences of financial decisions. By prioritizing such educational initiatives, society can cultivate future generations who approach personal finance with confidence and savvy, ultimately transforming how money is perceived and managed. Thus, engaging with young individuals equips them with essential skills, ensuring a ripple effect that can challenge and alter long-standing cultural norms.

Despite significant advancements, the conversation around personal finance still often centers on scarcity and fear rather than empowerment and opportunity. A shift in narrative can occur through intentional storytelling that emphasizes empowerment in overcoming financial challenges. Success stories of individuals who transitioned from debt to financial independence abound, providing relatable role models for those currently struggling. By framing financial crises not as insurmountable obstacles, but as catalysts for growth, communities can reshape their collective mindset. To encourage this shift, organizations can host local workshops featuring these narratives, inviting participants to share their experiences. As a closing exercise, readers could articulate their own financial goals and identify the steps they need to take to achieve them, reinforcing the notion that financial freedom is a reachable and worthwhile endeavor. Through community-driven initiatives, the cultural perception of finance can evolve into one that celebrates resilience and informed decision-making.

XVI. THE ROLE OF GOVERNMENT IN PERSONAL FINANCE

In navigating the complex landscape of personal finance, one might find themselves at a crossroads after facing a financial crisis. Take, for instance, Maria, a working mother of two who, like many, found her family teetering on the edge during an economic downturn. Governments play a pivotal role in such scenarios, stepping in to stabilize both individuals and institutions. Through direct financial aid, stimulus packages, and support programs, governments aim to alleviate the pressures that citizens face, ultimately fostering resilient households. This intervention is not merely a temporary fix; it creates a ripple effect that influences consumer confidence and spending habits. By providing safety nets, governments empower individuals like Maria to make informed financial decisions rather than succumbing to panic-induced choices. As we consider the broader implications of government support, we must remember that these programs are not just safety nets—they are launching pads for long-term financial independence.

Governmental policies and regulations significantly shape personal finance behaviors and standards. Policies that impact interest rates, tax incentives for saving, or regulation of financial products can alter individual financial trajectories. Consider the debt fueled life of Carlos, a recent college graduate burdened by student loans. He finds himself navigating a web of predatory lending practices often overlooked in an unregulated market. Through effective legislation, governments can mitigate these risks, ensuring that the financial system is equitable and accessible. This regulatory framework also fosters financial literacy, enabling individuals to grasp the nuances of budgeting, saving, and investing. Carlos, with the right government support and education, transitions from a cycle of debt to one of financial empowerment, illustrating the crucial role government plays not just in recovery, but in fostering a foundation for sustainable financial habits. At the heart of personal finance lies the concept of financial literacy, which government initiatives increasingly aim to enhance. Local workshops, online resources, and community programs have emerged to educate citizens on navigating their finances effectively. Imagine Jenny, a young entrepreneur who, after participating in a local government-sponsored financial literacy program, starts to apply principles from the RICH Method 2.0. With knowledge of reinvesting wisely and creating a solid safety net, she transforms her business strategy and personal finance management. Empowered by education, individuals can make informed choices that align with government initiatives aimed at fostering economic independence. This synergy not only uplifts individual lives but cultivates a culture of financially competent citizens. As readers look to improve their finances, reflecting on the resources available through government support can serve as the springboard for taking actionable steps toward financial freedom.

GOVERNMENT POLICIES POST-CRISIS

In the aftermath of any financial crisis, governments are often thrust into the role of both caretaker and architect, tasked with implementing policies that can stimulate recovery and bolster economic resilience. These strategies typically aim to address immediate economic damage while laying the groundwork for sustainable growth. The implementation of fiscal stimulus packages can provide much-needed relief to struggling families and businesses by boosting consumption and investment. Such measures have been shown to shorten the duration of recessions and reduce the long-lasting effects of economic downturns. Government policies must also be vigilant against creating dependency; the aim is to empower individuals and families, not to inhibit their financial independence. The key lies in designing initiatives that balance immediate economic relief with long-term personal finance education, thus encouraging individuals to take an active role in their financial destinies.

Surviving a financial crisis also compels policymakers to rethink how public services respond to citizen's needs, particularly concerning financial literacy. Many families, after witnessing their savings evaporate amid economic turmoil, often realize the profound gaps in their understanding of personal finance. Government efforts to implement educational programs that enhance financial literacy can be instrumental. These programs not only arm citizens with knowledge but also foster a culture of proactive financial planning. Consider a family that participated in a community financial workshop and subsequently learned about budgeting techniques and debt management strategies. Empowered by this newfound knowledge, they transformed their financial habits, leading to increased savings and improved credit scores. As policymakers focus on weaving financial literacy into the fabric of public education, they foster a generation of financially savvy individuals prepared for future economic challenges. The integration of technology into government policies post-crisis can play a pivotal role in propelling economic freedom. Digital platforms, increasingly adopted as tools for public service delivery, can streamline access to financial resources and assistance programs. By utilizing big data analytics, governments are able to identify vulnerable populations and tailor their support services more effectively. A single mother who once faced insurmountable barriers in accessing aid could now use a mobile app to navigate available resources effortlessly. This user-friendly interface turns what was previously a labyrinthine process into a straightforward experience, allowing her to focus on rebuilding her financial stability. By promoting technological solutions alongside traditional economic policies, governments can ensure that their initiatives serve not just to alleviate hardship, but also to foster an environment conducive to sustainable financial independence. As a practical step, citizens are encouraged to explore government-supported apps and platforms that can facilitate their journey toward economic empowerment.

SUPPORT PROGRAMS FOR INDIVIDUALS

Navigating through the aftermath of a crisis often requires individuals to access various support programs that can serve as lifelines during turbulent financial times. Consider a single mother in a small town who finds herself struggling to make ends meet after losing her job due to economic downturns. These support programs, including unemployment benefits, food assistance, and rental relief, provide much-needed resources to help individuals regain financial stability. By analyzing data on the uptake and effectiveness of these programs, one realizes that they're not merely temporary handouts, but stepping stones that allow individuals to invest in their own futures. Studies reveal that recipients of unemployment benefits are more likely to reinvest those funds back into their local economies, stimulating growth and fostering a sense of community resilience. As such, participation in these programs can be instrumental in transitioning individuals from dependency to independence.

The effectiveness of these support systems often hinges on awareness and accessibility. Imagine a scenario where someone is unaware of the assistance available to them due to inadequate outreach or complicated application processes. These barriers can amplify feelings of hopelessness and discourage participation in programs designed to help. Analysis of case studies shows that individuals who actively seek out and educate themselves about available support are frequently able to leverage these opportunities for personal and financial growth. In light of this, it becomes evident that programs must not only be established but also marketed effectively to reach those who would benefit the most. Increased collaboration between government agencies and grassroots organizations can facilitate a smoother transition into these support systems, empowering individuals to take charge of their financial futures.

The real power of these support programs lies in their ability to instill a mindset geared towards strategic financial planning. Picture a young entrepreneur who initially relies on small business grants following a crisis. Over time, the knowledge gained through this support transforms their approach to finances, encouraging a willingness to take calculated risks and seek alternative funding options. This narrative reflects a broader trend where individuals start to view support programs not just as handouts, but as educational opportunities that foster financial literacy. In doing so, they harness the principles of the RICH Method 2.0, integrating lessons learned into their financial strategies. The call to action is clear: individuals must engage with available resources, attending workshops or community meetings, to fully grasp the potential of these programs. This proactive approach can eventually lead to economic freedom, underscoring the vital role of support systems in a post-crisis landscape.

IMPACT OF REGULATIONS ON PERSONAL FINANCE

Navigating the landscape of personal finance often feels akin to crossing a treacherous pathway strewn with both pitfalls and opportunities. In this tense environment, regulations serve as both a safeguard and a hurdle for individuals seeking economic empowerment. On one hand, regulations are designed to protect consumers from predatory lending practices, ensuring transparency in financial transactions and creating a safety net for the most vulnerable. Regulations can also limit access to credit and investment opportunities, particularly for those with lower credit scores. A common scenario arises when aspiring entrepreneurs are turned away for loans due to stringent requirements, thereby stifling innovation and personal economic growth. As these regulations evolve in response to economic crises, individuals must stay informed and engaged, effectively balancing compliance and ambition. A practical exercise for readers is to assess their financial circumstances in light of recent regulatory changes, identifying both risks and opportunities to act upon.

Amid the intricate dance of personal finance and regulations, families often confront challenges that can feel overwhelming. Consider the story of Monica, a single mother striving to improve her financial standing while grappling with the complexities of her mortgage and credit card debt. Monica, like many, found herself impacted by the aftermath of the last financial crisis, which propelled her to reassess not only her savings strategy but also her understanding of legislative shifts in credit policies. Regulations aimed at making mortgage lending more responsible can sometimes inadvertently disadvantage those who need loans the most. While the tightened requirements were intended to reduce defaults, they simultaneously eliminated pathways for upward mobility for low-income earners. Readers are encouraged to reflect on their own financial decisions by charting out how regulatory frameworks have impacted their paths, ensuring they remain open to new possibilities for growth amidst restrictions. As individuals navigate these regulatory waters, the importance of proactive financial literacy becomes abundantly clear. This understanding empowers people to make informed decisions amid complex evolving laws. The contrast between successful savers and those continually struggling often lies in their grasp of financial regulations. Those who take the initiative to educate themselves on topics like tax benefits, credit score enhancements, and fiscal accountability will find themselves with an edge, opening doors that regulations may have initially seemed to close. The successful family-owned business that sought knowledgeable advisors to navigate small business regulations ultimately thrived, demonstrating that knowledge is as crucial as capital. Thus, it is imperative for readers to engage with financial education resources and consider integrating lessons from their financial experiences into their decision-making processes. As a call to action, readers could create a personal action plan that lays out key regulatory insights relevant to their financial goals, contributing to both personal empowerment and broader economic freedom.

Regulation	Impact
Dodd–Frank Wall Street Reform and Consumer Protection Act	Enhanced consumer protection and financial stability post-2008 crisis
Pension Protection Act of 2006	Increased automatic enrollment in 401(k) plans, leading to higher participation rates
Financial Literacy Education Requirements in High Schools	States mandating financial education saw a 1.5 % point increase in saving rates among individuals aged 30 to 49
Consumer Financial Protection Bureau (CFPB) Initiatives	Returned nearly $12 billion to 29 million consumers and imposed about $600 million in civil penalties over five years

Impact of Financial Regulations on Personal Finance

XVII. THE FUTURE OF PERSONAL FINANCE

In the wake of financial uncertainty, many individuals find themselves reflecting on their past decisions, often with a mix of regret and hope for change. This introspection is critical, particularly after a crisis that has reshaped our economic landscape. A recent study suggests that households, especially those hardest hit, are re-evaluating their spending habits and prioritizing savings more than ever. These revelations resonate with the experiences of everyday people. María, a single mother from Madrid, transformed her financial outlook by actively documenting her monthly expenses and seeking alternatives to her habitual purchases. She now reports a substantial increase in her savings, demonstrating that first steps toward financial literacy are often grounded in everyday choices. Hence, the future of personal finance is increasingly tied to a renewed focus on conscious spending and budgeting—central tenets of the RICH Method 2.0, which encourages individuals to embrace proactive financial habits. As the financial sector continues to evolve, technological advancements play a pivotal role in shaping personal finance practices. Digital banking applications and financial planning tools offer an unprecedented level of accessibility, allowing users to track spending in real time and set clear financial goals. This shift from traditional banking to digital platforms echoes the fiscal agility required in today's fast-paced environment. In interviews with financial advisors, many emphasize the importance of leveraging these technologies not only for tracking but also for educating users about sound financial practices. Jason, a financial advisor from Barcelona, describes how his clients are now more informed and engaged when it comes to their finances. They utilize apps that gamify saving and investing, fostering a sense of community and accountability. As these tools gain traction, it becomes evident that the future of personal finance will lean heavily on technology, making financial education more accessible and interactive than ever before. The concept of economic freedom often feels elusive, especially in the aftermath of a crisis that has left many financially vulnerable. Yet, embracing the RICH Method 2.0 presents an actionable pathway to reclaim that freedom. By focusing on reinvestment and purpose driven savings, individuals can cultivate financial independence that is not just a distant dream but an achievable reality. Practical exercises, such as journaling financial goals or creating a savings challenge, illustrate the methods core tenets and encourage self-reflection. Sarah, an entrepreneur from Valencia, shares her inspiring journey; after adopting these integrated strategies, she not only rebuilt her savings but also established a thriving business. This story exemplifies how financial literacy and disciplined habits create opportunities that pave the way for lasting economic freedom. As we look ahead, its crucial to engage actively in these practices, not just in theory but as part of daily life, thereby fostering a robust approach to personal finance for generations to come.

PREDICTIONS FOR THE NEXT DECADE

As we step into a new decade shaped by resilience and adaptability, individuals are increasingly prioritizing financial literacy. Consider María, a single mother navigating the financial landscape post-crisis. She dedicated herself to understanding budgeting and investing, transforming uncertainty into empowerment. Data indicate that over 60% of millennials prioritize financial education, with many seeking resources online and through community programs. They realize that knowledge is power, enabling better decision-making and investment choices. In this context, the RICH Method 2.0 emerges as a beacon, offering a structured approach to tackling personal finance with renewed vigor. By focusing on key principles—like reinvesting wisely—María learned to value her savings, investing them strategically in mutual funds rather than allowing them to languish in low-interest accounts. This narrative not only illustrates personal growth but also highlights a crucial societal shift towards valuing informed financial decisions.

Navigating the complexities of economic recovery post-crisis necessitates a deep dive into expenditure patterns. Take the story of Carlos, an entrepreneur who once succumbed to the culture of consumerism, racking up debt to maintain an image of success. Through the lens of the RICH Method, he recognized that improving expense efficiency wasn't merely about cutting costs; it was about reshaping his lifestyle. The emerging data reveal a 20% increase in consumers evaluating their spending habits more critically, challenging the cycle of impulse purchases fostered by societal pressures. Carlos embraced this shift, reallocating funds previously spent on unnecessary luxuries towards savings and strategic investments. This transition underlines the increased awareness about the long-term implications of spending. As individuals empower themselves financially, they not only enhance their economic stability but also contribute to a broader culture of financial responsibility.

The construction of a robust safety net stands out as a vital element in securing financial freedom. Consider the experience of Lila, who lost her job during an unexpected economic downturn. Initially paralyzed by fear, she quickly realized the importance of having accessible savings to navigate the crisis. Research underscores that over 40% of households lack sufficient emergency funds, emphasizing the often-overlooked necessity of a financial cushion. Lilas journey transformed her perspective on savings from a passive endeavor to an active strategy woven into her financial fabric. By harnessing purpose-driven saving, Lila aligned her savings goals with her personal values, instilling a sense of purpose in each dollar set aside. This approach not only buffered her during tough times but also motivated her to seek additional income streams. To foster such resilience, a practical exercise could involve creating a savings challenge where individuals commit to setting aside a small percentage of their income each month, reinforcing the principle of financial preparedness while cultivating a proactive mindset toward economic challenges.

2025	2026	2027	2028	2029	2030	Indicator
2.1%	2.1%	2.1%	2.1%	2.1%	2.1%	Real GDP Growth Rate
4.4%	4.4%	4.4%	4.4%	4.4%	4.4%	Unemployment Rate
1.9%	1.9%	1.9%	1.9%	1.9%	1.9%	Inflation Rate (PCE)
1.1%	1.1%	1.1%	1.1%	1.1%	1.1%	Federal Funds Rate
2.6%	2.6%	2.6%	2.6%	2.6%	2.6%	10-Year Treasury Note Yield

Projected U.S. Economic Indicators for 2025–2030

EMERGING TRENDS IN PERSONAL FINANCE

Navigating the aftermath of economic turmoil, many individuals find themselves reassessing their financial habits and priorities. In today's landscape, the emergence of digital financial tools plays a crucial role in this metamorphosis. Apps that cater to budgeting, saving, and investing offer unprecedented accessibility, allowing users to track expenses in real-time and make informed decisions on the fly. A recent study found that users of budgeting software reported a 25% increase in monthly savings. Herein lies an anecdote that illustrates this trend: Maria, a young professional burdened by student loans, discovered a budgeting app that not only helps her visualize her spending patterns but also encourages her to allocate a portion of her income to an emergency fund. As transformational as these tools are, it is essential to remember that technology alone does not guarantee financial literacy. The call to action is clear: leverage these tools to foster financial discipline while seeking education to underpin informed choices.

In tandem with the rise in financial technology, an increasing focus on sustainability in personal finance has emerged, reshaping how individuals approach their spending and investments. Gone are the days where financial success was measured solely by wealth accumulation; today, many are shifting toward values-based financial decisions that prioritize social and environmental impact. Consider the story of Thomas, an entrepreneur who decided to invest in renewable energy startups. His understanding of the dual impact— benefiting his portfolio while contributing positively to the environment—has shaped not only his financial success but also his identity. Recent data suggests that socially responsible investment funds have outperformed traditional funds, highlighting a potential reconfiguration of investment priorities in favor of sustainability. As this trend gains momentum, readers are urged to reflect on their values, reassess their investment strategies, and consider aligning their portfolios with their personal beliefs.

Another emerging trend is the increasing recognition of behavioral finance—specifically, understanding how emotions and psychological factors influence financial decisions. Amid the chaos of recent economic crises, individuals often find themselves trapped in cycles of fear and impulsivity related to their finances. An enlightening encounter with a financial psychologist revealed a common pattern: clients often make irrational decisions based on emotional responses rather than rational analysis. During economic downturns, people may rush to liquidate investments out of fear, missing opportunities for recovery. To counteract this instinct, it is pivotal to foster resilience and educate oneself on the psychological aspects of financial decision-making. Readers are encouraged to engage in reflective practices, such as journaling about their financial choices and the emotions behind them. This approach not only cultivates self-awareness but also prepares them to make more reasoned and adjusted financial decisions moving forward, thereby enhancing their overall economic freedom.

ADAPTING TO A CHANGING ECONOMIC LANDSCAPE

Navigating today's economic terrain is akin to balancing on a tightrope; every step requires mindful consideration of personal financial stakes. For many, this challenge brings to mind anecdotes of families who faced past recessions only to emerge with resilience and newfound wisdom. Take, for instance, Maria and Carlos, who were able to turn their financial plight around after making strategic decisions during turbulent times. They not only tightened their budget but also learned to embrace the importance of financial literacy. Collectively, their story highlights a significant trend: individuals who educate themselves about their finances tend to respond more adeptly to economic shifts. Yet, while the personal narrative brings a relatable flavor to their journey, the hard data reveals a sobering reality. Studies show that financial literacy directly correlates with the ability to navigate economic crises, underscoring the necessity of acquiring these skills as an essential aspect of personal finance.

As the global economy experiences rapid transformations, adapting to these shifts requires more than passive obedience to trends; it demands active engagement with sound financial strategies. An illustrative case comes from a family in Spain, who opted to rethink their expense priorities in light of rising living costs. By categorizing their expenditures and distinguishing between needs and wants, they not only managed to stabilize their finances but also cultivated a sense of control amidst uncertainty. Their experience illustrates the core tenet of the RICH Method 2.0: improving expense efficiency can serve as a reliable foundation. As engaging as these personal narratives are, they serve a dual purpose; they ground abstract financial concepts in relatable experiences, urging readers to take action. The pressing question emerges: how can one start to scrutinize their expenses today?

A practical exercise involving a simple spending diary can lay the groundwork for this transformative journey. The interplay between personal finance management and economic freedom suggests a crucial pivot: proactive measures are paramount to ensure financial stability. Anecdotal evidence often denotes that individuals who actively save and invest during downturns not only weather the storm but often find themselves better positioned in the aftermath. Consider the success story of a group of entrepreneurs who engaged in purpose-driven saving by investing in local ventures amidst economic uncertainty. This strategic foresight not only revitalized their community but also bolstered their personal financial standing, demonstrating the ripple effect of thoughtful financial choices. Herein lies the essence of the RICH Method 2.0; it empowers individuals to harness their savings towards measurable outcomes. It beckons readers to reflect on their motivations and consider engaging in a practical exercise by identifying a cause worth investing in, thus intertwining personal finance with broader economic welfare. Adapting to a changing economic landscape hinges upon a keen awareness of one's financial decisions and a commitment to lifelong learning.

XVIII. PRACTICAL EXERCISES FOR INTERNALIZING HABITS

Imagine standing in line at the grocery store, watching shoppers that seem to make effortless financial decisions, filling their carts with what appears to be the essentials while you mentally tally your monthly budget. The discomfort of financial insecurity often arises not just from a lack of funds, but from habitual mismanagement of resources. To counteract this, practical exercises aimed at internalizing habits can become crucial. One effective exercise involves implementing the "30-Day Rule," where individuals delay non-urgent purchases for thirty days. This simple act can shift ones mindset towards mindful spending, allowing for reflection on whether the desired item is genuinely necessary. By engaging in this practice, individuals report feeling more in control over their finances, which ultimately reduces impulsive spending habits that contribute to financial instability.

As stories unfold within communities struggling to regain financial footing after previous economic downturns, the concept of tracking expenses emerges as a transformative tool. Participants are encouraged to document every expenditure for a month, categorizing them into essentials and non-essentials. This exercise not only heightens awareness of spending patterns but also highlights areas where unnecessary expenditures can be trimmed. Interviews with financial advisors reveal that individuals who regularly engage in this activity are more likely to find additional savings, often rechanneling those into investments or savings. Real-life accounts of families who shifted from living paycheck to paycheck to building a modest investment portfolio illustrate the long-term impact of such habits. This exercise serves as a vital invitation to begin the journey towards economic freedom by confronting the reality of one's financial practices head-on. Building financial resilience requires not only awareness but also a consistent commitment to changing ingrained habits. One actionable strategy individuals can implement is the Automate to Save principle, which encourages setting up automatic transfers to savings accounts as soon as income is received. This exercise shifts the perspective from seeing saving as a leftover after spending to treating it as a prioritized expense. Success stories reveal that families who have adopted this habit often see their savings grow significantly without the mental burden of actively thinking about it. The efficiency of automating savings can ripple through an individual's financial behavior, fostering a proactive approach rather than a reactive one. Integrating practical exercises such as the 30-Day Rule, expense tracking, and automated savings into daily routines not only enhances financial literacy but also empowers individuals to take tangible steps toward achieving lasting economic freedom.

WEEKLY CHALLENGES FOR FINANCIAL DISCIPLINE

In the daily grind, financial challenges often go unnoticed until they reach a critical level. Consider the case of Laura, a single mother juggling work and family responsibilities. She found herself consistently overspending on groceries, a struggle compounded by a lack of clear budgeting. This common scenario underscores the importance of setting weekly financial challenges that promote discipline. By designating one week to tackle unnecessary expenses, individuals like Laura can identify spending leaks, such as impulse buys or premium brands, that stretch budgets thin. The act of tracking and re-evaluating expenses not only fosters awareness but also instills a sense of accountability, transforming financial management from a mere task into a proactive lifestyle choice. Such challenges serve not just as short-term goals but as foundational practices that lead to lasting financial habits, ultimately steering individuals toward the broader objectives of the RICH Method 2.0 framework.

Each week presents a new opportunity for growth, particularly when it comes to saving habits. Consider Greg, who, after years of living paycheck to paycheck, adapted to a challenge that asked him to save a percentage of his earnings every week. Initially daunting, this task became manageable when broken down into concrete steps. Greg started by saving just 1% of his weekly income and gradually increased this amount as his comfort level grew. This method of incremental change illustrates a vital principle of the RICH Method 2.0: sustainable financial practices are often built on small, consistent actions rather than drastic lifestyle overhauls. As Greg learned to prioritize saving, he also found creative ways to cut back on non-essential expenditures. This approach yielded not only enhanced financial security but also the empowerment that comes from recognizing ones capabilities in managing finances.

Weekly challenges can catalyze a transformation in perspective, reshaping how individuals view their finances. Take Sara, who initially approached her finances with a sense of dread, believing that budgeting was synonymous with deprivation. When she participated in a weekly savings challenge that encouraged small, purposeful expenses alongside larger savings goals, her mindset shifted. Sara began to see her finances as a tool for achieving her goals, rather than a burden. Through her daily assessment of spending habits and progress tracking, she identified areas to cut back without sacrificing enjoyment. By engaging directly with the practical exercises of setting limits on discretionary spending, Sara not only underscored her financial discipline but also cultivated a deeper sense of purpose in her saving strategy. This holistic engagement drives home a crucial lesson: financial stability is attainable when approached through manageable, bite-sized challenges that promote self-awareness and strategic planning.

SIMPLIFIED SPREADSHEETS FOR TRACKING

Picture a young couple, recently married and settling into a new home, staring at a cacophony of bills, receipts, and loan documents. In the face of this chaos, many often feel overwhelmed and unsure where to begin. Simplified spreadsheets can transform this daunting task into a manageable process, allowing individuals and families to systematically track income, expenses, and savings goals. These user-friendly tools enable users to categorize their financial transactions clearly, turning complex data into digestible information. By adopting a visually straightforward spreadsheet, our couple can swiftly identify where their money is going, prioritize essential expenses, and spot potential savings. As they engage with this streamlined approach, they develop a clearer picture of their financial health, thereby reducing anxiety and fostering proactive habits in their financial lives.

The power of simplified spreadsheets extends beyond mere organization; they also serve as an educational tool. By logging income and expenses consistently, users can gain critical insights into their spending patterns. With every entry in the spreadsheet, the couple becomes more aware of recurring costs, illuminating areas ripe for reduction or reevaluation. Testimonials from families who have previously battled debt highlight that this exercise often leads to the discovery of unnecessary expenses, such as subscription services that go unused. This realization can ignite a sense of agency and control over their finances. The ability to visualize their financial journey fosters an understanding of budgeting principles, which may have been previously unfathomed. As a collective learning experience, these spreadsheets encourage regular participation from all family members, ultimately reinforcing accountability and cooperation.

Implementing a practical exercise similar to this can revolutionize ones approach to finance. After establishing a simplified spreadsheet, users should commit to weekly reviews, allowing for an actionable reflection on both triumphs and challenges faced in pursuing economic freedom. Consider introducing a 'spending silence' week, whereby the couple refrains from discretionary purchases and focuses solely on needs. This period fosters mindfulness and provides valuable data for refining their tracking process. By conducting this review every weekend, users can assess patterns and trends over time, noting discrepancies or surprising insights. Encouraging this ongoing engagement not only solidifies financial habits but also seizes the opportunity for ongoing improvement. The consistent application of simplified spreadsheets fosters a deepened understanding of personal finance, empowering individuals to take definitive steps toward financial independence.

REFLECTIONS ON PERSONAL FINANCE JOURNEY

In the wake of financial upheaval, many individuals found themselves reassessing their economic choices amid a backdrop of uncertainty. The fallout from the crisis exposed common patterns in debt and spending that had long gone unchecked. Stories from families struggling to pay off credit cards or juggling multiple loans underscore a widespread mismanagement of finances. Interviews with financial advisors revealed that understanding one's cash flow is essential; by identifying unnecessary expenses, individuals can begin to reclaim their financial independence. This journey often begins with an uncomfortable confrontation with one's financial reality—one that encourages personal growth through reflection. By first assessing the mistakes made during the crisis, individuals can lay the groundwork for meaningful change. A practical exercise at this stage involves tracking spending habits for a month, empowering the individual to pinpoint exactly where financial adjustments can be made.

Transitioning from recognition to action, the RICH Method 2.0 emphasizes the importance of strategic reinvestment. By drawing on individual case studies, the essay illustrates how families recalibrated their financial priorities. Maria, a young mother, redirected her newfound savings into a diversified investment portfolio instead of habitual impulse purchases. Financial advisors advocate that creating a personalized reinvestment strategy is crucial not only for wealth accumulation but also for fostering economic stability. As data reveals an uptick in community investment initiatives, it becomes clear that reinvesting at a local level can instigate positive change, making economic freedom a collective endeavor. This is where the narrative invites readers to reflect and take action, perhaps by establishing a small monthly investment towards a meaningful goal or community project, thereby intertwining personal finance with societal contribution. The final chapter of personal finance transformation emphasizes the creation of a robust safety net, an often-overlooked aspect of economic independence. Creating emergency funds or insurance plans can seem daunting, yet compliance with expert financial advice suggests that these measures provide crucial buffers against adversities. Success stories abound, such as that of Jorge, whose discipline in saving led him to build a significant emergency fund, allowing him to confidently navigate job transitions. Relatable interviews reveal that many of those who prioritized safety nets subsequently experienced greater financial freedom and incidentally reduced anxiety about future uncertainties. The call to action here involves developing an incremental savings plan. Individuals can set realistic goals, diverting even a modest portion of their income into an emergency fund, thereby empowering them to face unexpected challenges with resilience and foresight.

XIX. THE IMPORTANCE OF DISCIPLINE IN FINANCE

Imagine sitting down to review your finances, only to find that your savings account has dwindled while credit card balances soar. This scenario is all too common, particularly in the wake of economic downturns. A critical truth emerges: discipline in finance is not a luxury but a necessity. Establishing a personal finance system grounded in disciplined spending and saving habits can dramatically alter one's financial landscape. Data reveals that individuals with strict budgeting practices and a commitment to regular savings outpace their peers in achieving economic stability. Families that adhere to the RICH Method 2.0 principles often report newfound financial confidence. Such discipline fosters an environment where informed decisions replace impulsive behaviors, and long-term goals become tangible milestones rather than distant fantasies.

In everyday life, the stories of individuals overcoming financial challenges illuminate the impact of discipline. Carlos, a single father, found himself drowning in debt while trying to support his two children after losing his job during the economic slump. He adopted the RICH Method 2.0 and redefined his approach to finances through disciplined spending and strategic saving. By creating a budget that prioritized essential expenses and setting aside a small percentage of his income for emergencies, Carlos regained control over his situation. His story not only showcases the transformative power of discipline but also serves as a reminder that even small, consistent efforts can yield significant results. Such narratives highlight that economic freedom is not merely about wealth accumulation; it is fundamentally about cultivating habits that support sustainable financial well-being.

As individuals reflect on their financial situations, it becomes essential to introduce practical exercises that reinforce disciplined financial habits. Start by tracking daily expenditures for a week to identify spending patterns and areas where habits can be improved. Engage in conversations about finances with family members or friends to foster accountability and support. These actions lay the groundwork for a more structured financial journey. Embracing discipline does not demand perfection; rather, it calls for progressive steps that cumulatively lead to a substantial impact. The journey towards economic freedom begins with an unwavering commitment to discipline in financial matters, paving the way for not only personal growth but also a resilient financial future.

BUILDING DISCIPLINE THROUGH HABITS

When reflecting on the trajectory of financial stability, it becomes evident that the threads of discipline and habit are intricately woven into the fabric of economic success. Everyday scenarios highlight the importance of small, consistent actions; for instance, consider the story of a recently married couple whose disorganized spending initially left them drowning in debt. Rather than succumbing to the overwhelming stress of their financial situation, they committed to forming a habit of tracking expenses on a daily basis. This simple yet impactful discipline reshaped their financial landscape, allowing them to identify unnecessary expenditures. As they developed this habit, they discovered that reinforcing their resolve through a visible budget not only curbed impulsive spending but also cultivated a deeper understanding of their financial priorities. Thus, the pivotal role of habit formation in building discipline asserts itself, acting as a foundation for effective financial management. Moving beyond anecdotal evidence, statistical insights further illustrate the profound impact of disciplined habits on financial health. Data reveals that individuals who engage in regular expense tracking are over 40% more likely to save effectively, as compared to those who do not. This striking correlation illuminates the broader implications of fostering discipline through habitual practice. As financial advisors frequently emphasize, the path to economic freedom does not lie in sporadic windfalls or risky investments but rather in the steadfast adherence to well-established routines. By cultivating habits such as daily financial reviews or weekly budget assessments, individuals can transform their financial circumstances from reactive chaos to proactive control. These practices are not merely suggestions but critical components of the holistic strategy outlined in the RICH Method 2.0, demonstrating how discipline in personal finance can breed both empowerment and resilience.

Concluding this exploration of habits and discipline, readers are encouraged to take their first practical step toward economic freedom by implementing a weekly financial check-in. This action serves as a bridge between theory and practice, allowing individuals to solidify their commitment to disciplined habits. The exercise is straightforward: allocate a specific time each week to review spending, assess savings goals, and adjust budgets as necessary. By establishing this pivotal habit, individuals can empower themselves to stay informed and make deliberate choices. The transition from uncertainty to clarity is gradual, yet the rewards are palpable—leading not only to informed financial decisions but also to sustainable economic freedom. As the stories of others who embraced this journey illustrate, the cultivation of discipline through consistent habits is a journey worth embarking upon, one that opens the door to a financially secure future.

LONG-TERM VS. SHORT-TERM THINKING

Imagine standing in line at a supermarket, cradling a cart full of items that represent both urgent desires and the rational need for financial prudence. This everyday scenario illustrates the tug-of-war between immediate gratification and long-term financial stability—a central theme in personal finance. Individuals often find themselves at a crossroads, where the allure of quick purchases conflicts with the disciplined choice of saving or investing for future goals. Short-term thinking may offer a momentary sense of satisfaction, but studies show that it can lead to detrimental debt accumulation and hinder the ability to build wealth over time. Conversely, a long-term perspective fosters better decision-making, enabling individuals to prioritize savings and investments that yield benefits in the future. Embracing the long-term view becomes essential, particularly in a post-crisis economy where sustainable financial practices are vital for recovery. As families emerge from economic adversity, the ripple effects of short-term thinking become increasingly evident. Many have faced tumultuous periods characterized by impulsive spending and inadequate savings, primarily driven by a lack of financial education and a desire for instant relief. Personal anecdotes reveal the struggles of individuals who succumbed to the quick fix mentality during the last major recession, often forcing them into a cycle of debt that felt insurmountable. Yet, those who managed to shift their focus toward long-term planning—such as creating emergency funds or investing in education—began to see more profound changes not only in their finances but also in their overall outlook on life. The narrative becomes one of empowerment as these individuals recognize the value of delayed gratification and the joy found in achieving long-term financial goals. This transition is not just a mental shift; it often requires re-evaluating one's entire approach to financial management.

To facilitate this shift, the RICH Method 2.0 emphasizes actionable strategies that bridge the gap between short-term desires and long-term aspirations. By incorporating practices like disciplined reinvesting and efficient expense management, individuals can create a sturdy safety net for future uncertainties. Real stories of families who diligently applied these principles highlight a transformation that is both impactful and relatable. One family, for instance, initially struggled with living paycheck to paycheck, but after implementing a long-term savings strategy, they achieved financial freedom that seemed unattainable before. As part of this analysis, readers are encouraged to reflect on their spending habits and see them through a new lens. By participating in practical exercises, such as tracking their monthly expenses or setting specific savings goals, individuals can begin to cultivate a mindset that prioritizes future security over fleeting pleasures.

Age Group	Objective Financial Knowledge	Subjective Financial Knowledge	Subjective Financial Management Ability
18–24	Positive association with both long-term and short-term financial behaviors	More strongly related to financial behaviors than objective knowledge	Less strongly related to financial behaviors compared to subjective knowledge
25–34	Positive association with both long-term and short-term financial behaviors	More strongly related to financial behaviors than objective knowledge	Less strongly related to financial behaviors compared to subjective knowledge
35–44	Positive association with both long-term and short-term financial behaviors	More strongly related to financial behaviors than objective knowledge	Less strongly related to financial behaviors compared to subjective knowledge
45–54	Positive association with both long-term and short-term financial behaviors	More strongly related to financial behaviors than objective knowledge	Less strongly related to financial behaviors compared to subjective knowledge
55–64	Positive association with both long-term and short-term financial behaviors	More strongly related to financial behaviors than objective knowledge	Less strongly related to financial behaviors compared to subjective knowledge
65 and older	More strongly related to long-term financial behaviors than subjective knowledge or subjective financial management ability	Less strongly related to financial behaviors compared to objective knowledge	Less strongly related to financial behaviors compared to objective knowledge

Financial Behaviors and Literacy Across Age Groups

SUCCESS STORIES OF DISCIPLINED SAVERS

Amid the challenging landscape of economic uncertainty, many find solace in the disciplined saving habits of others who have navigated similar storms. The story of Maria, a single mother from Valencia, illuminates the power of consistent savings. After experiencing the fallout of the previous recession, Maria began by setting aside just 10% of her monthly income into a separate savings account. Over time, her resolve allowed her to build an emergency fund that not only covered unforeseen expenses but also helped her balance the demands of single parenting and work. This straightforward yet impactful decision transformed her financial outlook, ensuring resilience against economic fluctuations. Despite initial reservations about restricting her spending, she found that disciplined saving fostered a sense of empowerment and control over her finances. To emulate Marias journey, consider establishing a similar savings bucket and committing to a percentage of your income, starting today.

Equally compelling is the narrative of the Gonzalez family, who turned their ordinary financial routine into an extraordinary success story through steadfast dedication to saving. Faced with mounting debt and an uncertain job market, they decided to challenge their spending habits by embarking on a year-long savings program. By meticulously tracking household expenses and targeting non-essential purchases, they managed to slash their monthly spending by 25%. This effort didn't just enable them to clear high-interest debts; it simultaneously laid the groundwork for their first investment in a small local business. Their discipline and collaboration as a family fostered an atmosphere of shared purpose, demonstrating the foundational principle of the RICH Method: harnessing purpose-driven saving. Inspired by their triumph, families everywhere can reflect on their spending habits and see where small adjustments can lead to significant financial improvements. The latest financial data reinforces the significance of such disciplined saving practices amid an ever-evolving economic landscape. Notably, the overall savings rate in Spain has seen notable fluctuations, reflecting both national trends and personal stories like those of Maria and Gonzalez. This dynamic highlights that while macroeconomic factors influence savings behavior, individual and family-level efforts are vital to achieving economic freedom. These success stories exemplify the long-term benefits of engaging with the principles of the RICH Method and demonstrate that financial stability is often rooted in persistent, disciplined actions rather than sudden windfalls. The consistent theme across these narratives is the call to action: by adopting straightforward savings strategies and setting defined financial goals, anyone can begin their journey toward economic independence, transforming challenges into opportunities for growth.

XX. THE ROLE OF MENTORS IN FINANCIAL SUCCESS

Navigating the labyrinth of personal finance can often feel overwhelming, particularly in a post-crisis economy where uncertainties loom large. Imagine a young professional, fresh out of college, striving to establish a foothold in their career while simultaneously grappling with student debt and a challenging job market. In situations like this, the role of a mentor becomes invaluable. The guidance from someone who has traversed similar financial hurdles provides not just wisdom but also practical strategies that resonate on a personal level. Mentors often share their own experiences of overcoming financial pitfalls, enabling mentees to identify potential mistakes before they occur. This anticipatory knowledge not only alleviates stress but also fosters a sense of confidence that propels individuals toward financial savvy. As aspiring individuals learn to reinvest wisely and improve expense efficiency, having a mentor to lean on can make the daunting journey of personal finance feel less isolating and more achievable.

Personal stories serve as poignant reminders of the impact mentorship can have on financial success. Consider an enterprising individual who once faced a mountain of credit card debt and daunting monthly payments. Through regular interactions with a seasoned financial advisor, this person learned to break down their expenses and identify wasteful spending. Armed with practical advice, they not only eliminated their debt but also began their journey toward saving for a first home. This transformation, spurred by mentorship, highlights a critical aspect of the RICH Method 2.0 framework: creating a solid safety net. Mentors provide not just knowledge but emotional support, helping mentees understand that financial freedom is a process built on incremental changes. The personal narratives embedded in these journeys emphasize the transformative power of mentorship, reminding others that with the right support, they too can emerge from financial hardship and prosper.

While the effectiveness of mentorship is apparent, it invites reflection on how individuals can strategically seek out these valuable relationships in their own lives. It can be through networking events, community groups, or even online platforms dedicated to personal finance education. As you embark on this journey toward economic freedom, consider establishing a mentorship connection as a proactive step. Identify areas of financial literacy that challenge you and actively seek out individuals who excel in those spaces. Engaging in dialogue and sharing experiences not only enriches your understanding but also strengthens your resolve to adhere to the RICH Method 2.0 principles. This approach empowers you to harness purpose-driven saving, ultimately fostering a sense of agency over your financial future. As a practical exercise, create a list of potential mentors, outlining qualities and experiences that you admire, and take the first step to reach out—your economic independence may depend on it.

FINDING A FINANCIAL MENTOR

Navigating the world of personal finance can often feel overwhelming, especially for those still reeling from the impact of recent economic crises. Imagine a young professional burdened by student loans and uncertain about making investment decisions, finding comfort in the advice of a seasoned financial mentor who once faced similar challenges. This relationship is not merely about acquiring knowledge; it's about leveraging lived experiences to demystify financial concepts and strategies. A mentor can provide invaluable insights derived not just from textbooks but from real-world triumphs and failures, guiding their mentee to avoid pitfalls they once encountered. By fostering an alliance built on personal anecdotes and data-driven advice, aspiring individuals gain the confidence to tackle their financial issues head-on, transforming anxiety into actionable steps toward financial stability.

In the pursuit of financial guidance, the focus should be on finding a mentor whose expertise aligns with one's unique financial situation. A family aspiring to buy their first home may benefit from a mentor who specializes in mortgage financing and real estate. Mentorship may also take the form of formal relationships through organizations or informal networks that facilitate these connections. The power of a mentor lies not merely in their knowledge but in their ability to personalize advice for the individual's circumstances, ultimately allowing for a more relevant application of strategies. As some mentors prioritize financial literacy, others focus on entrepreneurship or investment savvy, showcasing the diverse paths to economic freedom. Such tailored mentorship encourages individuals not only to improve their financial literacy but also to cultivate the discipline needed to execute sound financial practices.

As one reflects on the importance of mentorship, it becomes clear that the learning process is reciprocal. While the mentee gains knowledge and skills, mentors often find their perspectives enriched by fresh insights and renewed motivation. Picture a bustling online forum where mentors and mentees share struggles, victories, and resources, creating a community that thrives on cooperation and support. Identifying the right mentor thus becomes a strategic exercise; potential mentees should assess compatibility not just in terms of financial expertise but also shared values and backgrounds. Embarking on this journey means taking the first step in connecting with potential mentors, drafting targeted questions, and actively engaging in discussions on financial topics of mutual interest. This approach can reveal not only mentors but also a network of professional relationships that continue to inspire and strengthen financial literacy, ultimately moving closer to the goal of economic freedom after the crisis.

BENEFITS OF MENTORSHIP

Navigating the complex landscape of personal finance is often akin to venturing through uncharted territory; myriad pitfalls and daunting obstacles can leave individuals feeling overwhelmed. In this context, the role of mentorship emerges as a crucial lifeline. By forming relationships with seasoned mentors, individuals gain access to valuable insights and hard-earned wisdom that illuminate pathways to financial literacy and independence. These mentors often share their own stories of overcoming adversity, fostering an environment where mentees can acknowledge their fears and aspirations. A young entrepreneur might learn not only about effective budgeting strategies from a mentor but also about the emotional toll that financial decisions can take. This dual focus on practicality and personal growth amplifies the value of mentorship, enabling individuals to develop a well-rounded understanding of money management that transcends mere numbers.

The dynamic between a mentor and mentee often sparks transformative growth, both financially and personally. Mentorship encourages accountability, as mentors frequently check in on the financial goals of their mentees, pushing them to remain committed to their objectives. This relationship can foster a sense of community, reducing the isolation many feel when grappling with their financial decisions. Consider the story of a college student burdened by student loans who partnered with a financial advisor turned mentor. Together, they crafted a comprehensive repayment strategy informed by the advisors practical experiences during previous economic downturns. This not only empowered the student to tackle their debt with renewed vigor but also provided a unique framework to understand the emotional landscape of financial recovery. Through such narratives, the profound impact of mentorship becomes clear, illustrating how individual stories can intertwine with broader economic principles to foster resilience and strategic planning.

To fully harness the benefits of mentorship in achieving economic freedom, it is imperative to take proactive steps. Beyond merely seeking a mentor, individuals should actively engage in their learning process by articulating specific financial goals and challenges they wish to overcome. Engaging in proactive scenarios, such as organizing regular meetings or setting actionable tasks based on discussions with a mentor, can solidify the lessons learned. One could establish a routine of reviewing monthly expenses with their mentor, dissecting what changes can lead to improved spending efficiency. This practical exercise may not only culminate in financial insights but also strengthen the mentorship bond, creating a cycle of continuous feedback and improvement. As individuals embrace these structured interactions, they empower themselves and reinforce the idea that mentorship is not just about guidance; it is a dynamic relationship that cultivates sustainable economic freedom and self-awareness.

CASE STUDIES OF MENTOR-LED SUCCESS

In the shadows of economic uncertainty, many individuals find themselves grappling with mounting debts and financial instability. Consider Sara, a single mother in her thirties, whose reliance on credit cards spiraled into a staggering $15,000 debt after the last recession. Through sheer determination and guided by a financial mentor, she navigated her way to economic literacy. Her mentor's structured approach, rooted in the RICH Method 2.0 principles, emphasized the importance of reinvesting wisely. By reallocating her limited budget toward high-return savings vehicles—like a robust savings account—Sara successfully negotiated her debts down, fostering not just financial health, but also a renewed self-confidence. This personal journey illustrates a larger trend observed; mentorship empowers individuals to take tangible steps toward reinvesting in their financial future, breaking free from the suffocating cycles of debt that have plagued so many of their peers.

Diving deeper into the world of mentorship, the story of David, a recent college graduate, sheds light on the transformative power of financial guidance. After facing a precarious job market post-recession, David was left feeling adrift and uncertain about his financial prospects. His mentor, an established entrepreneur, introduced him to the concept of improving expense efficiency—a core tenet of the RICH Method 2.0. Through a series of candid discussions about budgeting, David recognized unnecessary subscriptions and adjustable spending habits that drained his finances. As he implemented these strategies, he not only managed to stabilize his finances but also began contributing to his retirement fund earlier than his peers. Davids experience resonates with many who reinvent their budgeting processes after seeking guidance, emphasizing how mentorship can illuminate paths previously obscured by financial chaos and uncertainty. The profound effects of mentorship extend beyond mere financial literacy; they also highlight the importance of creating a solid safety net for oneself and one's family. Take the Gonzalez family, whose story exemplifies a total turnaround after they engaged with a financial advisor who embraced the RICH Method 2.0s principles. Faced with an economic crisis that forced them to reduce their workforce, Gonzalez learned to harness purpose-driven saving. They established a robust emergency fund, steering their savings not just as a cushion against unforeseen circumstances but as a proactive approach to future planning. With their mentors ongoing support, they transitioned from a state of financial fragility to one of resilience, emphasizing both the emotional and practical benefits of mentorship. Their journey resonates deeply within communities impacted by financial crises, reminding readers that building a safety net is not just a dream but an attainable reality, especially when inspired by thoughtful guidance and relentless perseverance.

XXI. ADAPTING THE RICH METHOD FOR INDIVIDUAL NEEDS

In the pursuit of financial independence, many individuals encounter a myriad of obstacles that stem from a one-size-fits-all approach to personal finance. Imagine Maria, a single mother who juggles multiple jobs while striving to provide the best for her children. Her story illustrates a common struggle: generic financial strategies often overlook the unique circumstances of individuals like her. To address this gap, adapting the RICH Method for personal needs becomes paramount. By encouraging users to evaluate their own financial habits through the lens of their specific situations, the method invites a deeper understanding of personal finance. For Maria, this means prioritizing her limited resources efficiently while identifying the potential for reinvestment in her skills and education, ultimately breaking the cycle of financial instability. The initial step is to embrace a customized interpretation of the RICH Method, ensuring each individual can navigate their financial landscape with confidence and clarity.

Understanding personal financial goals also necessitates a shift in mindset, particularly in relation to expense management and saving strategies. Take the example of John, a recent college graduate buried under student loan debt and a meager salary. Faced with the daunting reality of his financial situation, he found himself overwhelmed by conflicting advice from various sources. The RICH Method's adaptability addresses this challenge by emphasizing the importance of recognizing one's financial identity and adjusting expense patterns accordingly. By integrating Johns story, we see the potential of the method to empower individuals to categorize their expenses into needs, wants, and savings. This triage allows for improved efficiency and encourages conscious spending and cultivating a safety net. For John, developing a practical budget using a simplified spreadsheet tool transforms his narrative from one of desperation to one of proactive engagement. Practical exercises become essential, enabling the implementation of tailored methods that convert theoretical financial wisdom into actionable strategies.

Cultivating an awareness of purpose-driven saving can fundamentally change how individuals perceive and accumulate wealth. Consider the case of Lisa, who initially viewed saving as an impossible task due to her high living expenses. By integrating the principles of the RICH Method, she learned to align her saving habits with her broader life goals, ultimately leading to a sense of empowerment and direction. Purpose-driven saving is not merely about setting aside money; it involves establishing a financial vision that resonates with personal aspirations. This shift requires moving beyond traditional savings accounts and exploring opportunities for reinvestment and growth, tailored to individual interests and circumstances. To transform her finances, Lisa engaged in a reflective practice, assessing her motivations and translating them into actionable savings plans. This narrative illustrates the importance of applying personalized techniques grounded in the RICH Method that catalyze shift from fear-driven savings to intentional financial growth. By embracing these approaches, individuals can take decisive steps toward achieving personal finance and, ultimately, economic freedom.

CUSTOMIZING THE METHOD FOR DIFFERENT PROFILES

Transitioning from a general understanding of financial principles to tailored strategies is crucial in addressing the diverse economic realities individuals face today. Consider Maria, a single mother working multiple jobs to support her family. Her financial landscape is markedly different from that of Carlos, a young professional with a steady income and no dependents. The success of the RICH Method 2.0 hinges on adapting its five-step system to fit distinct profiles like Maria and Carlos. By recognizing these nuanced financial situations, we can develop custom solutions that resonate more deeply with individual experiences, ultimately fostering a sense of ownership in the financial journey. The key lies in understanding that fluctuations in income, family responsibilities, and career aspirations create unique financial challenges. Thus, blending empirical data with personalized narratives ensures that the RICH Method is not just a theoretical framework, but a practical guide for varied profiles. Data-driven insights offer an invaluable lens for customizing financial methods. Recent statistics indicate varying savings rates among different demographics in Spain, revealing that younger adults tend to save less than their more established counterparts. Recognizing these patterns allows for the refinement of the RICH Method to engage younger audiences with relatable strategies, such as gamified savings challenges. Interviews with financial advisors often emphasize the importance of tailored advice, particularly for clients grappling with high levels of consumer debt. By integrating this knowledge, we can create relatable exercises that encourage participants to choose personalized approaches, such as debt snowball techniques or expense tracking, making the RICH Method not only relevant but also actionable. The inclusion of specific financial challenges fosters an environment where individuals feel empowered to actively participate in their financial growth.

To cultivate genuine engagement with the RICH Method, it is essential to provide practical exercises that align with each profiles unique challenges. Maria might benefit from workshops focused on budgeting for families, helping her prioritize essential expenses while considering emergency savings. Conversely, Carlos might find value in a mentorship program that connects him to seasoned entrepreneurs, fostering his understanding of investment possibilities. Each chapter concludes with tangible takeaway tasks that prompt readers to implement tailored strategies, such as creating personalized budget spreadsheets or committing to a week of mindful spending. These exercises serve not only to reinforce learning but also to motivate individuals to take deliberate steps toward enhancing their financial literacy. By ensuring that the RICH Method accommodates different financial profiles, we empower individuals to take actionable control over their economic futures, ultimately bridging the gap between knowledge and practice.

FLEXIBILITY IN IMPLEMENTATION

As financial landscapes shift in the aftermath of economic turmoil, the ability to adapt strategies is crucial. Consider the story of Maria, a single mother from Seville who found herself overwhelmed after job loss led to mounting debt. Faced with a harrowing financial reality, Maria began to apply principles from the RICH Method 2.0, discovering that flexibility in implementation was key to her turnaround. Rather than strictly adhering to a rigid budget, she adjusted her expense tracking to reflect her shifting priorities; this allowed for better management of unexpected challenges, such as emergency childcare costs. Such adaptability is not merely anecdotal; data shows that households that embrace a flexible approach to budgeting during crises tend to recover more rapidly. Maria's experience illustrates how a dynamic financial plan can serve the dual purpose of addressing immediate needs while laying the groundwork for long-term economic stability.

Flexibility in implementing financial strategies is not just about adjusting budgets; it encompasses a broader reevaluation of financial goals and methods. Take, for instance, Carlos, a small business owner who faced declining revenue after the pandemic. Initially, Carlos clung to his original business model, unaware of alternatives that could sustain him. Engaging with financial advisors, he learned to pivot his approach by embracing online sales and product diversification. This adaptability not only salvaged his business but also increased his savings. The RICH Method 2.0 champions such flexibility by encouraging individuals to reassess and realign their financial objectives continuously. Through hands-on exercises, households can learn to regularly evaluate expenditures and income streams, adapting their strategies in real-time. Resilience in financial planning thus emerges as a core tenet for achieving economic freedom in a post-crisis world.

The act of incorporating flexibility into personal finance strategies speaks to a broader cultural shift towards proactivity in financial management. Reflecting on her own journey, Laura, a recent college graduate, exemplifies how this flexibility fosters confidence. Initially overwhelmed by student loans, Laura committed to creating a side hustle aligned with her passions. By adjusting her initial financial plan to incorporate earnings from freelance work, she experienced a newfound sense of agency over her financial future. The RICH Method 2.0 encourages individuals to seek out creative solutions and opens the dialogue surrounding financial literacy, specifically highlighting the mental shift required to embrace change. With practical exercises accompanying each chapter, readers are invited to adapt these strategies to their unique circumstances, effectively making financial literacy an active and personalized pursuit. The call to action is clear: be flexible, be responsive, and take ownership of your financial journey.

EXAMPLES OF ADAPTATION IN REAL LIFE

Navigating the aftermath of a financial crisis often requires individuals and families to adjust to unexpected economic realities. Take, for example, Maria and Carlos, a couple grappling with mounting credit card debt after losing their jobs during the recession. In their efforts to regain financial footing, they utilized a fundamental aspect of the RICH Method 2.0: improving expense efficiency. By scrutinizing their monthly expenditures, they identified and eliminated non-essential services that quietly drained their budgets, such as subscription services and dining out. This conscious reallocation of funds allowed Maria and Carlos to funnel resources toward paying down their debts systematically. Their transformation reflects a broader trend; households across Spain reported an increased awareness of spending behaviors, with a noticeable uptick in budgeting apps and financial workshops. Adapting in this manner not only clears immediate debts but also elevates overall financial literacy, creating a foundation for lasting change.

As the economic landscape shifted, so too did consumer behavior, marking an adaptation not just in individual actions but in broader market trends. In the face of uncertainty, many individuals turned to entrepreneurship, spurred by necessity to fill gaps left by traditional employment. Javier, a former retail manager, pivoted to online tutoring when lockdowns shuttered physical classrooms. His story is echoed by countless others who adapted by leveraging their skills in innovative ways. Statistical data indicated a surge in self-employment ventures as people sought alternative income streams, showcasing resilience and creative problem-solving. This transition not only alleviated immediate financial strain for many but also contributed to a burgeoning gig economy that offers flexible opportunities. Such adaptability emphasizes the importance of harnessing ones strengths in uncertain times, an essential lesson in the pursuit of economic freedom after a crisis.

Cultivating a proactive approach to financial stability requires more than just reactive measures; it necessitates a mindset shift towards regenerative thinking and saving strategies. Families like the Torres family began focusing on purpose-driven saving— allocating funds specifically for their long-term aspirations, whether it be home ownership or securing their children's future education. They set tangible savings goals, transforming what once felt like a burden into a motivating vision. In response to economic pressures, statistics illustrate a marked increase in household savings rates, evidencing a communal pivot toward financial resilience. Practical workshops and online platforms emphasize how setting aside even a modest amount each month can lead to substantial safety nets over time. The Torres experience serves as a reminder that sustainable financial health is achievable through disciplined saving plans, encouraging others to embark on similar journeys toward economic independence. Each inspiring narrative concludes by urging readers to draft their saving goals today, thus commencing their path to financial empowerment.

XXII. COMMON PITFALLS IN PERSONAL FINANCE

Navigating the labyrinth of personal finance can be challenging, with many individuals unwittingly stepping into traps that can jeopardize their economic stability. One significant pitfall lies in the tendency to overlook budgeting. Without a conscious effort to track income and expenses, people often conflate their desires with their financial realities. A young professional may relish the excitement of a new luxury product but fail to consider the long-term implications of such a purchase on critical savings goals. Financial experts emphasize that establishing a budget is not merely a cautionary measure; it serves as a roadmap, illuminating where resources can be reallocated to prioritize savings and investments. Engaging in the budgeting process can also reveal spending patterns that warrant reassessment. As you reflect on your financial habits, consider initiating a weekly budget review, observing where discretionary spending could be redirected toward building your future financial security.

Another prevalent challenge arises from the pervasive culture of debt, particularly credit card debt. The allure of easy financing can lead to a false sense of security; however, without disciplined repayment strategies, individuals risk entering a cycle of escalating debt and financial stress. Many families, faced with unexpected expenses— be it home repairs or medical bills—resort to credit, spiraling further into financial strain. A striking case study involves a couple who believed they could manage their growing balances through minimum payments, only to discover that their debt was not diminishing; it was compounding. This narrative brings to light the necessity of developing a robust approach to debt management, which includes applying strategies such as the snowball or avalanche methods for repayment. To address this challenge, take a moment to assess your current debt situation and consider setting a realistic goal to reduce it by a specific percentage by year-end.

The lack of sufficient financial education emerges as a critical barrier to personal finance success. Individuals often enter the workforce ill-equipped to make informed decisions regarding savings, investments, and retirement planning. As a result, they may remain stagnant, allowing opportunity costs to accumulate. A poignant story is that of a devoted public school teacher who, despite years of service, struggled to save adequately for retirement. Many professionals find themselves in similar positions, realizing too late that a lack of understanding can greatly hinder their financial growth. This underscores the importance of seeking continuous learning opportunities—whether through workshops, online courses, or financial literacy podcasts. As a proactive step, commit to reading one finance-related book each month, or participate in a local financial workshop to enhance your understanding of personal finance. Each small step can significantly influence your future financial landscape, driving you closer to economic independence.

IDENTIFYING COMMON MISTAKES

In the aftermath of the last major economic recession, many individuals found themselves grappling not just with financial distress but with a lack of awareness regarding critical money management principles. A young couple recently interviewed described their struggle with accumulating credit card debt, which ballooned during the crisis, largely due to impulsive spending and a failure to communicate effectively about finances. This scenario is a common illustration of how emotional decision-making often superseded rational financial planning. The trap of overspending on non-essentials, fueled by the convenience of credit, often leads to a cycle of debt that feels insurmountable. Recognizing these patterns is crucial, as it lays the groundwork for adopting smarter financial habits. Analyzing these mistakes allows individuals to pinpoint where they might have gone wrong, fostering a more critical approach to their spending habits and an awareness of the emotional triggers driving them toward financial instability.

Increasing awareness of common financial pitfalls also involves examining the patterns of debt accumulation that typically emerge in times of economic uncertainty. Data reveal that a significant percentage of families experienced increased reliance on loans and credit during the crisis, illustrating a misguided belief in temporary fixes rather than lasting solutions. One interviewee recounted how a personal loan meant to cover emergency expenses quickly became a long-term burden. Such decisions reflect a broader societal trend where consumers opt for quick relief at the expense of financial health. Addressing this mistake requires a shift toward more proactive financial planning, such as creating acute awareness of the total debt picture and understanding interest rates and repayment terms. This focused approach helps individuals to develop a strategic mindset around borrowing and lending, allowing for better management of financial resources and diminishing future crises.

Practicing disciplined financial behavior also includes a concerted effort to bridge gaps in financial education, which is often the root cause of many fiscal missteps. Many individuals enter adulthood without the essential knowledge of budgeting, investing, or even basic financial literacy, leading to steep learning curves during times of hardship. An example from a local community workshop illustrates how attendees gained confidence by engaging with practical budgeting exercises, transforming vague financial knowledge into actionable steps. The exercise not only highlighted their previous oversights but also empowered participants to adopt effective money management strategies. By committing to continuous learning and applying newfound skills in real time, individuals can turn past mistakes into stepping stones toward economic freedom. Readers are encouraged to seek out local resources, workshops, or online tutorials that focus on building strong financial foundations, as the journey to financial stability often begins with a solid understanding of personal finance.

Mistake	Impact
Lack of Financial Knowledge	60% of adults with limited understanding of credit and personal finance have made financial mistakes costing $1,000 or more. Among Gen Zers and Millennials, 29% and 38% respectively report losses of $5,000 or more due to inadequate financial knowledge.
Excessive Spending on Housing	50% of Americans spend more than 30% of their household's gross monthly income on rent or mortgage payments, exceeding the recommended 28% threshold.
Carrying High-Interest Credit Card Debt	Nearly 50% of credit cardholders carry a balance, with 18% accruing balances of $10,000 or more. Carrying a $2,000 balance at an 18% interest rate could take 24 years to pay off with minimum payments.
Not Having an Emergency Fund	Without an emergency fund, unexpected expenses can lead to high-interest debt or missed payments, causing financial stress.
Ignoring Credit Reports	81% of consumers do not check their credit reports, potentially missing signs of identity theft or errors that could affect credit scores.

Common Financial Mistakes and Their Impact

STRATEGIES TO AVOID PITFALLS

In the wake of a financial crisis, many individuals found themselves grappling with the consequences of unwise spending and poor debt management. Imagine a single parent, diligent in their work yet overwhelmed by rising costs, succumbing to high-interest loans just to make ends meet. This scenario is all too common in the aftermath of economic upheaval, where the allure of quick-fix solutions can lead to a cycle of financial instability. To navigate these murky waters, one of the most effective strategies involves diligent tracking of expenses—even the seemingly insignificant ones. In doing so, individuals can unearth patterns that expose unnecessary expenditures, allowing for budget modifications that not only relieve immediate pressure but set the foundation for healthier financial habits. Such tactical adjustments are not just about cutting costs; they are about fostering an awareness that empowers individuals to reclaim control over their finances and avoid the traps that ensnared them previously.

As families begin to prioritize their financial literacy, the value of seeking professional advice becomes increasingly apparent. Consider a couple who, after witnessing their friends fall prey to predatory lending practices, took the initiative to consult a financial advisor. Through their diligence and informed decision-making, they learned to differentiate between sound financial strategies and those riddled with pitfalls. Engaging with experts, these families were able to navigate complex financial landscapes while establishing a robust savings plan tailored to their unique situations. This proactive approach underscores the importance of committing to education in personal finance; it bridges the gap left by traditional schooling. By equipping themselves with knowledge, individuals not only fortify their immediate fiscal situations but also develop long-term strategies that promote sustainable economic freedom, curating pathways that others can follow. The essence of avoiding financial pitfalls lies in cultivating a mindset geared toward resilience and adaptability. Each financial misstep serves not merely as a risk but as an opportunity for growth. A recently unemployed individual, faced with dwindling savings, embarked on a journey of reinvention, leveraging their skill set to create an online business. Such narratives highlight the breath of creativity and determination that can flourish in the face of adversity. Practical exercises, such as goal-setting frameworks and adaptive budgeting techniques, provide structured ways for individuals to visualize their aspirations while preparing for contingencies. By embracing a holistic approach to financial health that combines personal anecdotes with tactical strategies, individuals can navigate uncertainties with confidence. Through this blend of foresight and resilience, the pathway not only to avoid pitfalls but also to achieve genuine economic freedom reveals itself.

Intervention Strategy	Description
Systems Navigation and Access	Assisting individuals in understanding and accessing financial support systems.
Financial Literacy and Skills	Providing education on financial management to enhance decision-making.
Emergency Financial Assistance	Offering immediate financial support to address urgent needs.
Asset Building	Encouraging savings and investments to build financial security.
Employment and Educational Support	Facilitating access to job opportunities and educational resources.
Affordable and Accessible Transportation	Ensuring reliable transportation to employment and essential services.
Housing	Providing stable and affordable housing options.

Community Intervention Strategies to Reduce Financial Strain

LEARNING FROM OTHERS' MISTAKES

Imagine a vibrant café bustling with patrons sipping lattes, each engrossed in their own financial dilemmas. Amid the clinking of cups, a middle-aged couple shares their story of financial distress, exposing how ignoring the lessons from past economic downturns led them down a precarious path. The Great Recession laid bare the dire ramifications of poor financial decisions; from overspending on luxury items to flippantly ignoring the necessity of saving. By examining these missteps, individuals can actively avoid similar pitfalls, learning from the experiences of others rather than waiting for personal disaster to unfold. The café's regulars nod in agreement, reflecting on their own encounters with debt and inadequate financial literacy. It's evident that understanding collective mistakes creates a foundation for better decision-making and highlights the importance of financial education as a necessary precursor to wealth creation.

As the conversation at the café deepens, it becomes apparent that many people fail to recognize the patterns of overspending and risky investments. The stories shared resonate with the stark reality found in economic data—over 70% of individuals lack a clear personal finance strategy. Interviews with financial advisors reveal that most clients approach them only in crisis mode, often after accruing significant debt. This knee-jerk response underscores a avoidable trajectory: had they actively learned from previous economic missteps, they might have developed informed strategies for wealth accumulation and risk management. The narrative here is clear; by studying the financial blunders of others, individuals can design proactive approaches to their finances. Instead of becoming another cautionary tale, learning from the past equips people with the knowledge to forge a path toward stability and wealth.

To turn these observations into actionable strategies, one need only look around. Just as the café crowd draws on anecdotes and collective experiences, readers can implement the RICH Method 2.0 to restructure their financial futures. The steps—Reinvesting wisely, Improving expense efficiency, Creating a solid safety net, and Harnessing purpose-driven saving—serve as essential guides drawn from real-life transformations. By setting aside a few hours each week to analyze personal spending habits against these principles, individuals can shift their financial trajectory. Keeping a simple expense log can illuminate unnoticed patterns—whether its weekly takeout or impulse purchases—that drain savings. At the heart of learning from others is the realization that change begins with self-reflection and disciplined action. The cafés patrons leave that day not only energized but also equipped to rewrite their financial stories, avoiding the common pitfalls that so many have stumbled upon before.

XXIII. THE INTERSECTION OF PERSONAL AND SOCIAL RESPONSIBILITY

In the aftermath of the last recession, many individuals found themselves grappling with unprecedented financial uncertainty, illuminating the delicate balance between personal actions and broader societal responsibility. Picture a family struggling to meet monthly mortgage payments, their anxiety reflecting broader economic trends that forced entire communities into hardship. Their story is not unique; it resonates with statistical data highlighting rising rates of mortgage delinquency and stagnating wages. This intersection of personal finance and social responsibility is characterized by a shared burden. When individuals lean into personal financial improvement, they inadvertently contribute to the stabilizing of social structures. Understanding this symbiotic relationship encourages individuals to view their financial decisions as part of a larger narrative—one that can foster economic resilience among their peers.

While personal responsibility in managing finances is crucial, it is essential to recognize how societal frameworks influence those choices. Consider the first-time entrepreneur who, inspired by anecdotal stories of success, takes a leap of faith only to encounter institutional barriers that stifle growth. Data suggest that economic mobility is often affected by factors such as access to financial education and community resources. This discrepancy underscores why it's essential to cultivate an environment that empowers all individuals to develop sound financial practices. When families share their success stories, whether through overcoming debt or achieving savings goals, they inspire a ripple effect that encourages others within their communities. This narrative emphasizes the importance of social structures in supporting personal endeavors, creating an atmosphere where everyone can thrive together.

Bridging personal and social responsibility involves actionable steps that empower individuals and communities alike. As you reflect on your financial habits, consider the lessons learned from others in your community who have adopted the "RICH Method 2.0." Imagine workshop sessions focused on building a budget or sharing experiences about managing debt effectively—these gatherings can foster connections that bolster societal well-being. As a practical exercise, take time to engage with peers through informal discussions on financial challenges and victories. Such initiatives can shift perspectives, illustrating that personal finance is not solely an individual endeavor but an opportunity to uplift others. In doing so, you contribute to a more financially literate society, ultimately achieving not just individual prosperity, but collective economic freedom in the face of adversity.

FINANCIAL DECISIONS AND SOCIAL IMPACT

The lasting effects of past economic downturns have reshaped how individuals approach financial decisions today. During the last major recession, countless households faced not only personal financial ruin but also the broader social issues that arose, such as increased unemployment and rising inequality. In many cases, these struggles borne from mismanaged finances were compounded by a lack of education surrounding financial literacy. Families who relied heavily on credit found themselves entangled in debt cycles, disproportionately affecting lower-income communities. The lessons learned through such trials underscore a pivotal shift in how individuals can view their financial decisions as not just personal choices but as contributors to greater social dynamics. By recognizing this interconnectedness, individuals become motivated to adopt more responsible financial behaviors that ultimately benefit both their household and the wider community. A compelling exercise for those looking to make an impact might involve assessing one's spending habits and identifying areas where conscious changes can foster stronger economic resilience.

As households embrace the principles of the RICH Method 2.0, a transformation manifests not just financially but socially. The method weaves together crucial elements— Reinvesting wisely, Improving expense efficiency, Creating a solid safety net, and Harnessing purpose-driven saving—that extend beyond profit margins to cultivate community well-being. Families applying these strategies may choose to prioritize local businesses in their reinvestment practices, thus fueling neighborhood economies. By improving expense efficiency, individuals can redirect their savings towards community initiatives, such as educational programs or local charities, establishing a cycle of giving that supports both personal and communal growth. Real-life anecdotes illustrate this phenomenon, where one family's decision to save a portion of their budget for local volunteering not only reduced their overall expenses but also strengthened community ties. This blend of discipline and social awareness lays the groundwork for an approach to finance that champions economic freedom while nurturing a vibrant social fabric.

Looking at the macroeconomic landscape, personal financial decisions increasingly reflect broader societal trends. With data showing a shift in saving behaviors across demographics, families are becoming more mindful of how their actions shape the economic environment around them. In Spain, for example, a rising savings rate among younger adults signifies a departure from previous spending habits, suggesting a growing awareness of the long-term impact of their financial decisions. Interviews with financial advisors reveal a trend toward socially responsible investing, where individuals seek not only returns but also alignment with their values in economic pursuits. This movement fuels discussions about the importance of financial education within communities, serving as a catalyst for collective economic improvement. The essence of exercising financial agency, therefore, lies in understanding how personal choices reverberate throughout ones community. To drive this home, readers may engage in a weekly challenge: identify a financial decision that could empower both themselves and their community, reinforcing the idea that personal finance is intrinsically linked to social impact.

RESPONSIBLE INVESTING

Imagine a young couple, Laura and Miguel, grappling with mounting student debt while also looking to invest for their future. Their story reflects a common dilemma faced by many: how to build a prosperous financial future while remaining socially and environmentally conscious. Responsible investing serves as a beacon for individuals like Laura and Miguel, guiding them away from traditional investment paths that often prioritize profit over purpose. By choosing investments that align with their values—such as renewable energy companies or socially responsible funds—they can contribute positively to society while still aiming for financial returns. This dual approach appeals to a growing demographic of investors, as evidenced by rising trends in Environmental, Social, and Governance (ESG) investing, which prioritizes long-term sustainability over short-term gains. The key realization is that financial freedom doesn't have to come at the expense of ethical concerns; rather, the two can coexist harmoniously.

As we delve deeper, consider the staggering statistics emerging from various surveys that indicate a significant shift in the mindset of contemporary investors. More than half of millennials and Generation Z now view responsible investing as a critical factor in their financial planning. The current economic landscape necessitates a departure from speculative investments that are susceptible to market volatility. For many, responsible investing not only serves a moral imperative but also presents a viable long-term strategy to mitigate risks. Interviews with financial advisors reveal that clients increasingly demand transparency about the social and environmental impact of their investments. The narrative is evolving from sheer profit maximization to a more nuanced understanding of the ramifications of financial choices. This evolution is a crucial aspect of the RICH Method 2.0, emphasizing that investors have the power to influence their financial outcomes while making a meaningful difference, thus promoting a sense of economic freedom rooted in responsibility.

Building a responsible investment portfolio, however, can appear daunting for those unfamiliar with the financial terrain. To demystify this process, it's important to take practical steps that can be applied immediately. Individuals should begin by educating themselves on ESG metrics and green funds available in the market. This knowledge equips investors to make informed choices rather than relying solely on traditional stock recommendations. Consider creating a simple spreadsheet to track potential investments, noting their ethical ratings and the sectors they represent. For Laura and Miguel, this exercise not only allowed them to align their finances with their values but also created a concrete plan for investment. Responsible investing exemplifies a proactive approach to personal finance; it furthers economic independence and encourages individuals to become stakeholders in a better future. This practical tool serves both as an educational exercise and a call to action, inviting others to take the first step on their responsible investing journey.

COMMUNITY ENGAGEMENT THROUGH FINANCE

In neighborhoods across urban and rural landscapes alike, the spirit of community is often illuminated through shared financial aspirations. Individuals frequently rally around collective goals, whether they are pooling resources to create local businesses or engaging in community-based investment schemes. Such initiatives reflect an understanding of finance that transcends the individual, illustrating the profound implications of economic collaboration. Data suggests that communities that actively interact with their local economies see an increase in job creation and a decrease in unemployment. Yet these statistics only scratch the surface; behind them lie narratives of families who have experienced transformation through collaboration. A group of suburban residents pooled savings to purchase a local grocery store, increasing access to fresh food and generating jobs for community members. The mobilization of financial resources has not just empowered families but also enhanced their social fabric, highlighting that when individuals unite, they can erect a resilient economic foundation.

In navigating the lessons from past financial crises, it becomes evident that education in financial literacy must extend beyond traditional methods and focus on community engagement. Many families emerge from economic downturns carrying scars of debt and uncertainty; however, proactive sharing of financial knowledge within communities provides a beacon of hope. Community workshops, often led by experienced facilitators, not only distribute information but also cultivate dialogue about money management practices. These interactions can demystify complex financial concepts, fostering an environment where participants feel equipped to make informed decisions. As families begin to share their stories—both successes and failures—they contribute to a shared narrative that disarms the stigma surrounding financial hardships. The result is a collective intelligence that empowers individuals to challenge the status quo, nurturing a sense of responsibility towards both personal and communal financial health.

As communities embrace innovative strategies grounded in financial collaborations, the prospect of economic freedom emerges as a tangible goal. The RICH Method 2.0 underscores a systematic approach to personal finance that can be collectively adopted. By focusing on reinvestment, expense efficiency, safety nets, and purpose-driven savings, individuals are prompted to think not in isolation but as active participants in a larger economic ecosystem. Consider the single mother who joined a financial cooperative with her neighbors; by pooling resources for saving and investing in local businesses, she not only improved her financial standing but reinforced community ties. Simple yet empowering exercises, such as tracking savings for communal projects, can extend financial engagement beyond individual practices. As communities implement these steps, they might find that economic resilience reinforces social bonds, creating environments where wealth distribution is not just possible, but a shared journey. The call to action is clear: engage with your community to fortify both personal and collective financial futures.

XXIV. EVALUATING SUCCESS IN PERSONAL FINANCE

Navigating the turbulent waters of personal finance often starts with an intimate understanding of one's own economic behavior. For many, daunting debt levels and impulsive spending patterns emerged as byproducts of the last economic crisis. Take the case of María, a single mother who once found it virtually impossible to maintain her finances amidst rising living costs. By carefully examining her spending habits, she identified that a significant chunk of her budget was absorbed by small, frequent purchases, largely driven by emotional gratification rather than necessity. This realization reflects a larger trend, where personal finance education remains scarce, leaving individuals unaware of their financial missteps. Evaluating success in personal finance requires not just an assessment of numbers, but also an emotional audit—understanding the motivations behind spending behavior can pave the way for a more disciplined financial approach. To transform one's economic health, individuals can start recalibrating their spending habits and documenting daily expenses to identify leaks in their finances.

In the quest for economic freedom, improving expense efficiency has emerged as a pivotal step in evaluating personal finance success. Many individuals, like John, a recent college graduate, initially underestimate the impact of their fixed expenses, such as rent and utilities. After conducting a thorough assessment, John discovered that relocating to a more affordable area could not only release a significant portion of his income but also accelerate his savings goals. This story serves as a powerful reminder that success in personal finance is intrinsically linked to the ability to scrutinize and optimize recurrent expenditures. Engaging with data on average living costs can offer further enlightenment; for instance, analyses of local housing markets can unveil potentially life-changing opportunities for savings. Tapping into local insights equips individuals to make informed decisions that enhance their financial standing. Readers should grasp the importance of scrutinizing their expense patterns and consider conducting a bi-monthly review of their financial commitments to foster a more stable economic future.

The creation of a solid safety net is essential for financial resilience, particularly in the wake of crises, which often expose vulnerabilities in individual financial planning. Consider Alicia's experience: after unexpectedly losing her job during the economic downturn, she realized that her meager savings could hardly cover her expenses. Alicias situation underscores the critical need for a structured approach to savings, particularly an emergency fund that can absorb at least three to six months of living expenses. Yet, it is not merely about having a cushion; it is about cultivating the habit of prioritizing savings as a non-negotiable expense. By regularly diverting a portion of her income toward her safety net, she not only regained her financial footing but also developed a sense of security and independence. To effectively build an emergency fund, individuals should initiate a monthly savings challenge, designating a specific percentage of their income towards this goal. In doing so, they take proactive steps toward achieving lasting economic freedom, transforming the shock of crisis into an engine for future growth.

METRICS FOR MEASURING FINANCIAL SUCCESS

In the midst of financial uncertainty, many individuals find themselves grappling with an overwhelming sense of confusion regarding their financial health. Are they truly making progress, or merely treading water? This dilemma can be alleviated by establishing meaningful metrics for measuring financial success, which serve as essential benchmarks for personal and entrepreneurial growth. One pivotal metric is the savings rate, which acts as an indicator of how much income is set aside for future use. A family may realize that by simply adjusting their budget, they can increase their savings rate from 10% to 15%. This practical adjustment not only provides a more secure financial footing but can also bolster confidence in achieving longer-term goals, such as purchasing a home or funding a child's education. Individuals are encouraged to calculate and track their savings rate regularly, fostering a sense of accountability while moving toward economic freedom.

Understanding debt-to-income (DTI) ratios can transform personal finance from a daunting task into an attainable goal. The DTI ratio, which compares total monthly debt payments to gross monthly income, offers a vivid snapshot of financial health. A lower ratio indicates that one is within a comfortable range of debt, while a higher ratio may signal the need for immediate changes. A young entrepreneur might discover that their DTI ratio hovers around 45%, which raises red flags for potential lenders. Through calculated financial discipline, such as reducing unnecessary expenses and strategizing debt repayment, they can aim to lower their DTI within a few months. This shift not only enhances one's credit profile but also paves the way for future investment opportunities. Individuals should routinely assess their DTI and seek to improve it, working to eliminate debt burdens that inhibit their quest for economic stability.

Assessing net worth provides a comprehensive view of one's financial journey, encapsulating assets and liabilities in a single figure that gauges overall economic health. Consider a middle-aged couple evaluating their net worth after unexpectedly losing their jobs during the last crisis. By carefully tracking and analyzing their assets—such as retirement savings, home equity, and investments—against their liabilities, they gain crucial insights that inform their financial decisions moving forward. This holistic picture can reveal areas for improvement and help prioritize saving or investment plans. To maintain momentum on the road to economic freedom, individuals should commit to reviewing their net worth regularly, using it as both a motivator and a guidepost for setting and achieving ambitious financial goals. Engaging in this practice not only empowers individuals but encourages a proactive mindset conducive to lasting financial success.

Metric	Description	Calculation
Revenue	Total income generated from sales of products or services before expenses are deducted.	Revenue = Sales Price × Units Sold
Net Income	Profit remaining after all expenses and taxes are subtracted from revenue.	Net Profit = Revenue – Total Expenses
Cash Flow	Net amount of cash being transferred into and out of a business, indicating liquidity.	Operating Cash Flow = Net Income + Non-Cash Expenses – Increase in Working Capital
Gross Profit Margin Ratio	Percentage of revenue remaining after deducting the cost of goods sold, indicating production efficiency.	Gross Profit Margin Ratio = (Revenue – COGS) / Revenue × 100
Profit Margin Ratio	Percentage of revenue remaining after all expenses, taxes, and costs have been deducted, indicating overall profitability.	Profit Margin Ratio = (Revenue – Expenses) / Revenue
Quick Ratio	Measures a company's ability to meet its short-term obligations with its most liquid assets.	Quick Ratio = (Cash + Marketable Securities + Accounts Receivable) / Current Liabilities
Accounts Receivable Aging	Measures the average number of days it takes for a company to collect payments from customers.	Accounts Receivable Aging = (Accounts Receivable / Total Credit Sales) × Number of Days
Accounts Payable Aging	Measures the average number of days a company takes to pay its own invoices.	Accounts Payable Aging = (Accounts Payable / Total Credit Purchases) × Number of Days
Break-even Point	The sales amount—in either unit or revenue terms—at which a business neither makes a profit nor incurs a loss.	Break-even Point = Fixed Costs / (Sales Price Per Unit – Variable Cost Per Unit)
Composite Financial	A measure of an institution's financial health, combining multiple financial	CFI = (Primary Reserve Ratio + Viability Ratio + Net Operating

Index (CFI)	ratios to assess overall stability.	Revenue Ratio + Return on Net Assets Ratio) / 4

Key Financial Metrics for Assessing Financial Success

CELEBRATING SMALL WINS

Every individual has experienced moments of light amid darker times—those small victories that brighten the path to financial stability. Imagine a single mother juggling her job and her children, who sets aside a modest $20 from her weekly paycheck. It may seem trivial compared to the overwhelming expenses she faces, yet this act is a pivotal shift in her financial mindset. By recognizing and celebrating such small wins, individuals can foster a sense of accomplishment that reinforces their commitment to long-term financial goals. These incremental successes provide the motivation needed to tackle larger challenges, especially in the aftermath of a crisis where financial uncertainty looms large. The act of journaling these small achievements can transform abstract goals into tangible milestones, empowering individuals to persist despite setbacks. In the context of the RICH Method 2.0, appreciating these small victories is essential for sustainable change. Data suggest that individuals who regularly celebrate their minuscule accomplishments are more likely to achieve significant financial objectives. A couple who systematically track their savings progress not only reduces their credit card debt more efficiently but also cultivates a healthier relationship with money. These seemingly minor victories act as instant feedback, encouraging continuous engagement with their financial journeys. The emotional impact of recognizing small wins often translates into behavioral changes, fostering a proactive approach to managing expenses. This cycle of recognition and action is particularly key in environments accustomed to financial fluctuation, highlighting that even incremental progress should be acknowledged.

As readers navigate their financial pathways post-crisis, focusing on small wins can serve as a grounding strategy to cultivate resilience. Imagine setting aside a few minutes each week to reflect on financial accomplishments, no matter how minor they may appear. Perhaps someone found an extra $10 in their budget, or they successfully resisted an impulsive purchase. Engaging in this reflective practice not only builds confidence but also reinforces the notion that every step toward financial well-being is significant. The power of small victories lies not just in their quantity but in their ability to change mindsets—transforming anxiety about money into proactive financial habits. To harness this approach effectively, readers are encouraged to create a "small wins" ledger, documenting their achievements to serve as a source of inspiration and motivation on their journey toward economic freedom.

LONG-TERM VERSUS SHORT-TERM SUCCESS

Navigating the financial landscape often entails a critical conversation about how individuals prioritize their financial goals. Recent data shows that many families are leaning toward short-term success, often opting for immediate gratification over long-term planning. This inclination is not merely psychological but rooted in a societal culture that glorifies quick wins. Personal stories abound, such as that of a working mother in Barcelona who, overwhelmed by daily expenses, frequently resorts to credit for immediate needs rather than saving for her children's future education. This reliance on short-term solutions can illuminate the pitfalls associated with forsaking long-term financial stability, as many fail to recognize the compounding benefits that prudent investments and thoughtful savings can yield over time. As we dissect this behavioral pattern, its pivotal to stress the importance of shifting perspectives from immediate returns to those that build a safer, more sustainable financial future.

As we delve deeper into the concept of long-term success, it becomes clear that the rewards of patient financial management are manifold. Research indicates that individuals collaborating on a long-term financial plan often achieve greater economic freedom and resilience against market fluctuations. Reflecting on real-life encounters, a retired couple in Valencia shared their journey of living frugally but deliberately, which led them to save for a comfortable retirement. By prioritizing investments over impulse purchases, they not only fortified their financial standing but also set an inspiring example for their community. Such narratives highlight the contrast between short-term satisfaction derived from immediate purchases and the lasting benefits of foresight and planning. Herein lies the call to action: individuals must evaluate their spending habits, not just in terms of satisfaction, but through the lens of how those habits will shape their futures.

Bridging the gap between short-term actions and long-term financial goals necessitates cultivating a mindset that values economic discipline. The RICH Method 2.0 emphasizes the necessity of creating a solid safety net, which acts as a buffer against unforeseen crises—a lesson learned harshly during economic downturns. Engaging with tangible financial exercises can demystify this process for those hesitant to embrace a strategic approach. Families are encouraged to reassess their budgets and redirect even a modest monthly allocation towards an emergency fund or investment account. In doing so, they transform not just their financial reality, but their financial literacy, turning the daunting task of savings into manageable steps. For every short-term decision made, consider the long-term implications, ensuring that each choice contributes toward building a legacy of economic empowerment.

XXV. REFLECTING ON THE JOURNEY TO ECONOMIC FREEDOM

The journey to economic freedom is often fraught with obstacles, yet the path becomes clearer when individuals focus on actionable steps rooted in real-life experience. Many people find themselves overwhelmed by the remnants of financial crises, grappling with complicating factors such as high debt and low savings rates. These challenges can seem insurmountable, but stories of those who have changed their financial outlook illuminate the possibilities. One such example is Maria, a single mother of two, who, after facing eviction, turned her life around by employing the principles of the RICH Method 2.0. Her transformation highlights the importance of addressing personal financial education gaps and empowers readers to think critically about their own circumstances. By recounting her struggle and eventual triumph, Maria serves as a relatable figure that encourages others to engage with their finances actively, paving the way for a journey toward secure economic footing.

As individuals like Maria take actionable steps to navigate their economic pitfalls, it becomes essential to spotlight the foundational principles that steer them. The RICH Method 2.0 offers a structured framework that encourages one to reinvest wisely, improve expense efficiency, create a solid safety net, and harness purpose-driven saving. Each of these components is intricately designed to address everyday financial missteps, such as impulse buying and underestimating the significance of an emergency fund. Real-world data on savings rates and labor market trends corroborates these strategies, revealing a correlation between mindful financial practices and visible economic improvement. A recent study highlighted that families adopting systematic budgeting habits experienced a significant increase in monthly savings. Thus, by integrating personal narratives with quantitative evidence, readers can appreciate the profound impact of a disciplined financial approach, rendering the concept of economic freedom not merely an abstract goal but an achievable reality.

In closing, embarking on the journey to economic freedom requires not only aspiration but also tangible action steps that can lead to lasting change. The stories of individuals who have implemented the RICH Method 2.0 serve as powerful testament to the possibility of transformation. For those ready to take the plunge, new habits await to be cultivated: assessing expenditure patterns, setting up automated savings, and seeking out resources for financial literacy. The final call to action beckons readers to evaluate their current financial status to identify areas needing improvement. A practical exercise or challenge, such as tracking weekly spending or developing a basic budget, can ignite that first spark of change. By marrying personal anecdotes with practical steps that others have taken, the narrative encourages a community of individuals empowered to change their economic destiny, effectively turning aspirations into accomplishments.

PERSONAL GROWTH THROUGH FINANCIAL MANAGEMENT

Amid the daunting landscape of economic uncertainty, many individuals find themselves at a crossroads, grappling with financial insecurities that were accentuated during the last significant recession. These personal struggles often trigger a profound internal awakening, prompting a reevaluation of priorities and methods of financial management. Anecdotal experiences highlight how families emerged from this turbulence by confronting their fiscal habits head-on. An interview with a financial consultant reveals that emotional resilience can be directly linked to one's financial literacy; those who took control of their budgets reported greater satisfaction in their lives. The RICH Method 2.0 encourages this proactive mindset, challenging individuals to not only recognize the damage caused by poor fiscal choices but to also embrace the growth that comes from implementing systematic changes in their financial attitudes. The first step towards personal growth, therefore, lies in transcending fear and acknowledging the power of informed financial decision-making. Identifying and rectifying common financial pitfalls can facilitate a transformative journey toward economic freedom. Many families discovered that their previous approaches lacked transparency and efficiency, leading to unnecessary debt accumulation and missed opportunities. Through real-life case studies, the essay illustrates how the insights gained from analyzing one's spending habits can unveil underlying motivations and reveal practical strategies for enhancement. A single mother juggling multiple jobs shared how adopting the principles outlined in the RICH Method 2.0 not only helped her gain control over her expenses, but also empowered her to save for her children's future. This dual benefit of immediate financial relief and long-term sustainability becomes a driving force for personal growth, creating a ripple effect that fosters hope and confidence. The act of revisiting ones financial history serves as a cornerstone for building a resilient economic framework.

The journey towards financial mastery is underscored by a commitment to continuous self-improvement. By harnessing the tenets of the RICH Method 2.0, individuals can cultivate an adaptive mindset that prioritizes reinvestment and purpose-driven savings. Regular assessments of one's financial health can lead to dynamic changes, allowing for an agile response to fluctuating economic landscapes. Families who participated in workshops organized around these principles noted a significant shift in their financial habits and attitudes. They engaged in hands-on exercises that encouraged accountability and collaboration, leading them to not only achieve personal milestones but also to support one another in their endeavors. As external pressures shift, the call to action remains clear: commit to consistent, reflective practices in financial management. Sustainable economic freedom is attainable, rooted in the belief that personal growth is intrinsically linked to informed, purposeful choices in money management.

THE ROLE OF RESILIENCE IN FINANCE

Amidst the uncertainty of financial markets and unexpected crises, resilience emerges as a pivotal quality for individuals seeking economic stability. Consider the story of Nina, a single mother whose world turned upside down during the last recession. While grappling with mounting bills, she channeled her determination into applying a structured approach to her finances. Through budget adjustments and calculated investments, she was able to not only survive but thrive post-crisis. Such personal narratives underline the importance of resilience, which goes beyond mere persistence; it encompasses adaptability and innovation when navigating financial challenges. Data supports this necessity for resilience, revealing that individuals who embrace a proactive mindset during economic downturns are more likely to recover and enhance their financial standing. This understanding empowers readers to cultivate resilience, transforming potential setbacks into stepping stones for future prosperity.

Transitioning from personal anecdotes to broader implications, one cannot underestimate how resilience shapes collective financial behavior. Statistics illuminate a remarkable trend: households that adopt resilient financial strategies are increasingly better prepared for economic shocks. These families prioritize savings and reduce impulsive spending, fostering an environment of security and preparedness. In interviews with financial advisors, a common theme emerges: the ability to pivot and reassess spending habits is crucial. Families that cut unnecessary expenses during tough times not only safeguard against future crises but also improve their overall financial literacy. This collective shift toward resilient financial practices serves as a catalyst for broader economic recovery, suggesting that fostering such qualities can enhance community stability. As readers reflect on their financial journeys, the takeaway becomes clear: adapting and learning to bounce back lays the groundwork for more secure economic futures. For those eager to harness resilience in their financial pursuits, practical steps can turn this conceptual framework into concrete action. Begin by evaluating current spending habits and identifying areas for potential savings. Frequent assessments of monthly expenditures, whether through digital tools or traditional budgeting spreadsheets, can reveal patterns in spending that could be modified for increased efficiency. Encourage a mindset shift; rather than viewing obstacles as insurmountable, approach them as opportunities for growth and learning. To foster a resilience-focused environment, consider forming support groups with peers who share similar financial goals. By regularly discussing challenges and successes, individuals can reinforce a shared commitment towards economic freedom. This interactive approach encourages a continuous cycle of improvement and accountability, paving the way for a financially free and resilient future.

SHARING YOUR STORY WITH OTHERS

In the wake of financial upheaval, many individuals find solace and strength in the experiences of others. When families share their stories of hardship and resilience, they create an invaluable resource for those navigating similar challenges. Consider Maria, a single mother who, after losing her job during the last recession, turned to budgeting workshops in her community. Not only did she develop the discipline required to manage her limited resources, but she also connected with others, discovering new strategies to increase her savings and reduce unnecessary expenses. This social interaction highlights a critical aspect of the RICH Method 2.0: the emphasis on community. Personal narratives, bolstered by statistics showing a direct correlation between shared experiences and financial literacy, demonstrate how collective knowledge can empower individuals to make informed choices. The act of sharing creates a support network, fostering resilience among those striving for economic freedom.

The transformative power of storytelling is also evident in structured financial mentoring programs, where participants refine their skills through shared experiences. When clients discuss their financial journeys, advisors can personalize guidance, tailoring advice to resonate with their unique situations. Take Jamal, who articulated his struggles with debt and the emotional weight it brought. His openness encouraged a conversation about mindful spending and the importance of establishing a solid safety net. Empirical evidence reinforces this approach, revealing that storytelling not only enhances learning but also solidifies commitment to change. By integrating personal anecdotes into financial discussions, individuals may find actionable strategies that fit their lifestyles. This method not only demystifies complex financial concepts but also holds participants accountable, ensuring they remain engaged in their financial journeys. As an integral component of economic empowerment, sharing financial experiences can foster actionable change in personal finance education. Each narrative, laden with triumphs and setbacks, serves as a catalyst for self-reflection and motivation. Vanessa, who turned her financial woes into a blog detailing her budgeting journey, inspired countless readers to confront their own financial habits. Such stories, rooted in deep emotion and practical lessons, remind individuals that they are not isolated in their struggles. The statistics indicating a rise in financial literacy among those who engage with personal finance communities can be a compelling call to action. To harness this potential, consider participating in a local financial workshop or starting a discussion group focused on personal finance. Reflecting on one's own journey can not only illuminate personal pathways to economic freedom but also inspire others to take the first step in their own financial transformation.

XXVI. CONCLUSION

Navigating the turbulent waters of personal finance in the aftermath of a global crisis presents both a challenge and an opportunity. Many individuals have found themselves grappling with the lessons of the past, recognizing that the same financial missteps can lead to recurrent hardships. By analyzing the experiences of others who have faced similar dilemmas, it becomes apparent that adherence to systematic approaches, such as the RICH Method 2.0, can radically change their financial landscape. A family that made a conscious effort to reassess their budget not only improved their savings rate but also discovered opportunities for investment that they previously overlooked. This narrative of transformation underscores an essential truth: the journey to economic freedom is often shaped by proactive engagement, disciplined saving, and informed decision-making, rather than sheer good luck or market fluctuations.

Understanding that the pandemic catalyzed shifts in financial behavior and economic landscapes is pivotal. Data showed that many households increased their savings during lockdowns, not merely out of necessity but from a newfound awareness of financial resilience. This collective behavior offers a backdrop to evaluate how individuals can build a robust financial foundation. By exploring real-life testimonies, we can see the profound effects of restructuring one's financial priorities. An entrepreneur who repurposed their business model amidst adversity illustrates the resilience and adaptability that the RICH Method emphasizes. These firsthand accounts serve as powerful reminders that achieving economic freedom is not just a theoretical goal; it is a practical reality that can be realized through determination and structured planning.

The path to financial stability is undeniably influenced by past crises, yet it also encourages a reexamination of one's financial practices through the lens of learned experiences. The RICH Method 2.0 stands as a beacon for anyone eager to transcend their financial challenges. By actively engaging with practical exercises and committing to a disciplined approach, individuals can reshape their financial futures. As they implement changes in areas such as expense management and savings strategies, they not only secure their economic well-being but also foster a sense of empowerment and control over their lives. Encouraging readers to undertake their own financial audits or to develop personalized savings plans will solidify the insights gained throughout this exploration, proving that with mindful application, economic freedom is not just an aspiration but a reachable goal.

SUMMARY OF KEY POINTS

Navigating through the financial uncertainties following a crisis often entails more than just recovering lost ground; it is about reshaping our entire approach to personal finance. Many individuals fall into the trap of repeating previous mistakes, such as overspending or failing to prioritize savings, which only perpetuates their struggles. The RICH Method 2.0 emerges as a strategic framework designed to guide people through this perilous landscape. By integrating practical data—like the growing savings rate in Spain and lingering high mortgage debt levels—this method delivers a structured way for individuals to reassess their financial situations. It's not just about dry statistics; real families offer insights into how they adapted these strategies to enhance their economic resilience. As readers absorb these stories, they are encouraged to reflect on their financial habits through tailored exercises, setting the stage for real, actionable change. A key pillar of the RICH Method 2.0 is improving expense efficiency, a concept that resonates deeply with many who find it challenging to balance their budgets. Consider a working mother who juggles her career and family responsibilities, often relying on convenience products that quickly drain her funds. By introducing simplified budgeting methods and expense tracking, she begins to uncover significant savings simply by planning meals and utilizing bulk buying strategies. This approach not only curtails frivolous expenditures but also fosters a mindset shift towards informed spending. Anecdotes from financial advisors reinforce this transformation, emphasizing that behavioral changes in spending can result in substantial increases in savings and investments. Readers are prompted to undertake similar exercises in their own lives, ultimately turning what seems like a formidable task into a manageable, step-by-step process towards financial empowerment.

Harnessing the power of purpose-driven saving is where emotional engagement meets tactical finance. Many individuals may save money, but do so without clarity on their financial objectives, leading to stagnant accounts and demotivated savers. The RICH Method 2.0 emphasizes that understanding one's personal goals—be it a new home, education for children, or retirement—can invigorate the saving process. A relatable story shared in this context is of an entrepreneur who, after experiencing a major financial setback, refocused his energy on explicitly defining his aspirations. This clear vision propelled him to save strategically and invest wisely, resulting in a robust financial portfolio. The method advocates for reflective exercises that help readers identify personal goals, linking them directly to their saving habits. In closing chapters, practical frameworks for tracking these goals are provided, reinforcing the idea that financial freedom is within reach, crafted through intentional saving and purposeful planning.

CALL TO ACTION FOR READERS

Navigating the complexities of personal finance can often feel like a daunting endeavor, especially in the wake of economic uncertainty. Imagine the feeling of overwhelm as bills pile up and the pressure to make sound financial decisions grows. Yet, it is precisely these moments that can serve as catalysts for transformative change. The RICH Method 2.0 offers a structured approach to reclaiming control over one's financial landscape. By systematically dissecting spending habits, assessing savings potential, and re-evaluating financial priorities, individuals can carve out a path toward economic freedom. Whether it's a family reevaluating its budget after losing a job or an individual learning to navigate debt better, the method allows for personalized application. Accepting the challenge to outline current financial behaviors sets the stage for actionable improvement—allowing readers to confront their economic realities head-on.

As you dive into the specifics of reinvesting wisely and improving expense efficiency, personal reflections emerge as powerful motivators. Consider the experience of a single mother who, after a period of financial strife, began to categorize her monthly expenditures. This simple act of listing expenses illuminated previously overlooked spending patterns, propelling her towards a more streamlined financial approach. Implementing the RICH Method not only provided her with tools but also instilled a newfound confidence that she could take command of her finances. Realizing that the initial discomfort of analyzing one's financial situation can yield substantial benefits serves as a compelling call to action. By committing to weekly financial reviews, individuals can systematically shift their mindset and gradually transform their financial standing, paving the way for greater security and stability.

The journey toward economic independence is fundamentally about fostering resilience and purpose-driven saving. Picture a recent college graduate, burdened by student debt yet eager to start anew. By embracing the RICH Method's principles, such as creating a solid safety net and focusing on savings tied to long-term goals, she begins to build an actionable plan that resonates with her values. It is essential for readers to understand that taking small but deliberate steps, like setting aside even a modest percentage of their income, can lead to substantial leaps toward financial wellbeing. To truly embody this journey, take a moment to draft a personalized savings plan that aligns with individual aspirations and daily realities. This exercise not only invites accountability but also fosters a sense of agency—ultimately cultivating the foundation for lasting economic freedom and independence in uncertain times.

FINAL THOUGHTS ON ECONOMIC FREEDOM

In reflecting on the economic upheavals of recent years, it becomes increasingly clear that moments of crisis often serve as catalysts for transformative thought. Many individuals emerged from the last recession with a newfound understanding of financial resilience, learning the hard way how pivotal economic freedom is in safeguarding personal well-being. Consider Maria, a single mother from Madrid who faced job loss and mounting bills. Through her journey, she discovered that economic freedom is not just about having a well-paying job; it's also about managing debt wisely, prioritizing savings, and cultivating a mindset that embraces opportunity rather than fear. By adopting the principles of the RICH Method 2.0, she not only stabilized her finances but also fostered a sense of agency over her economic future—a valuable lesson that reinforces the importance of understanding and actively pursuing personal finance as a pathway to freedom. The economic landscape is often shrouded in complex data trends that can seem daunting, but they reveal critical insights into the workings of personal finance. As highlighted by Spain's fluctuating savings rates and alarming levels of mortgage debt, economic behavior directly impacts personal freedom. Many individuals continue to struggle with misconceptions about budgeting and financial planning despite an abundance of information. Interviews with financial advisors reveal that the real issue is not a lack of data but rather a lack of actionable steps that individuals can take. They emphasize the importance of understanding ones financial situation fully, paving the way for better decision-making that aligns with ones goals. Acknowledging this gap, the RICH Method 2.0 encourages readers to break down their financial habits into manageable parts, starting with simple exercises that foster awareness and confidence. This foundational step can dissolve the intimidation often experienced when confronting finances head-on. As we consider the road ahead, the notion of economic freedom becomes more than just an abstract concept; it transforms into a practical guide for navigating financial landscapes. The RICH Method 2.0 underscores the necessity of creating a solid safety net while harnessing a purpose-driven approach to saving. Here lies a compelling invitation: imagine transforming modest savings into a robust safety buffer that empowers you to seize new opportunities without jeopardizing your economic stability. Envision yourself deliberately channeling your efforts into understanding where your money goes and re-evaluating your spending habits. As this journey unveils opportunities for greater financial health, individuals will find empowerment not just in accumulating wealth but in the freedom to make choices that align with their life's purpose. Take the time to assess your financial landscape today, set achievable goals, and apply the practical exercises recommended in the RICH Method 2.0 to embark on your journey to economic freedom.

ENCOURAGEMENT FOR CONTINUED LEARNING

In the aftermath of economic instability, the pursuit of financial stability often feels daunting. Yet, there exists a transformative power in continued learning that can turn despair into actionable insight. Imagine a single parent, grappling with unpaid bills and soaring costs, who stumbles upon a free online course about personal finance. Initially skeptical, this individual gradually discovers techniques for budgeting, debt management, and savings that were previously elusive. As they absorb new information, the financial fog begins to clear, leading to smarter choices and a subtle shift in mindset. This narrative reflects a broader trend: data indicates that those who engage in ongoing financial education are more likely to manage their resources effectively. Thus, by encouraging continual growth in financial literacy, not only do we build resilience, but we also empower individuals to reclaim their economic lives amidst adversity. The challenge lies in seeking out resources and committing to small steps that enrich financial knowledge.

A key feature of the RICH Method 2.0 is its emphasis on understanding personal finances through practical, real-world examples. Consider the story of Maria, an entrepreneur who faced crippling debt after the previous recession. Instead of succumbing to hopelessness, she enrolled in a series of workshops focused on expense efficiency, sparking a fundamental change in her approach to financial management. Maria's experience underscores the significance of peer learning environments; in sharing struggles and strategies with others, individuals not only learn but also feel less isolated on their journeys to economic freedom. This interconnectedness highlights the importance of community in education. As financial anxiety lingers post-crisis, fostering an atmosphere of shared learning becomes essential.

Encouragement from peers can serve as a powerful motivator, urging individuals to take bold steps toward mastering their finances and harnessing their potential for success.

To fortify the foundation of one's financial knowledge, it is crucial to take concrete actions that steer behavior into a positive trajectory. Each chapter of the RICH Method 2.0 culminates in exercises designed to reinforce learning. Imagine setting aside thirty minutes each week to assess your financial habits, tracking expenses, or exploring investment options. Such practical undertakings not only solidify the lessons learned but also build a sustainable practice of financial mindfulness. By incorporating these exercises into daily routines, individuals can cultivate a mindset that welcomes continual learning as part of life. Whether it's listening to a podcast on economic trends or engaging with a financial advisor, these small yet significant choices shape one's journey toward economic resilience. The key takeaway is clear: encourage yourself to view learning as an endless path. Richer knowledge leads not only to personal satisfaction but also to financial independence in an ever-evolving economic landscape.

BIBLIOGRAPHY

Krish Kandiah. 'Home for Good.' Making a Difference for Vulnerable Children, John Murray Press, 3/14/2013

Health and Medicine Division. 'Communities in Action.' Pathways to Health Equity, National Academies of Sciences, Engineering, and Medicine, National Academies Press, 3/27/2017

Charlotte C. Hamilton. 'Her Money, Her Rules.' A Woman's Guide to Financial Freedom, eBookIt.com, 1/28/2025

Kate Levinson, Ph.D.. 'Emotional Currency.' A Woman's Guide to Building a Healthy Relationship with Money, Clarkson Potter/Ten Speed, 4/12/2011

Charlene Walters. 'Launch Your Inner Entrepreneur: 10 Mindset Shifts for Women to Take Action, Unleash Creativity, and Achieve Financial Success.' McGraw Hill Professional, 2/23/2021

Morgan Housel. 'The Psychology of Money.' Timeless lessons on wealth, greed, and happiness, Harriman House Limited, 9/8/2020

Trenton Williams. 'Learning from Entrepreneurial Failure.' Emotions, Cognitions, and Actions, Dean A. Shepherd, Cambridge University Press, 3/4/2016

Stuart L. Hart. 'Base of the Pyramid 3.0.' Sustainable Development through Innovation and Entrepreneurship, Fernando Casado Caneque, Routledge, 9/8/2017

Karen Firestone. 'Even the Odds.' Sensible Risk-Taking in Business, Investing, and Life, Routledge, 10/14/2016

Gregory K. Ericksen. 'Women Entrepreneurs Only.' 12 Women Entrepreneurs Tell the Stories of Their Success, John Wiley & Sons, 4/26/1999

Daniel C. Finley. '101 Advisor Solutions: A Financial Advisor's Guide to Strategies that Educate, Motivate and Inspire!.' Lulu.com, 12/1/2011

Robert B. Olshansky. 'After Great Disasters.' An In-depth Analysis of how Six Countries Managed Community Recovery, Laurie A. Johnson, Lincoln Institute of Land Policy, 1/1/2017

Dave Ramsey. 'Financial Peace.' LAMPO, 9/1/1995

Jing Jian Xiao. 'Handbook of Consumer Finance Research.' Springer International Publishing, 5/30/2018

Aleksandra Grzesiuk. 'Financial Literacy and Financial Education.' Theory and Survey, Beata Świecka, Walter de Gruyter GmbH & Co KG, 3/18/2019

Manuel London. 'Continuous Learning in Organizations.' Individual, Group, and Organizational Perspectives, Valerie I. Sessa, Psychology Press, 6/3/2015

Castro-Santos, Laura. 'Financial Management and Risk Analysis Strategies for Business Sustainability.' Enríquez-Díaz, Joaquín, IGI Global, 4/2/2021

Nikos Mourkogiannis. 'Purpose: The Starting Point of Great Companies.' Macmillan, 8/19/2008

Susan B. WILSON. 'Goal Setting.' How to Create an Action Plan and Achieve Your Goals, Michael Dobson, AMACOM, 3/12/2008

Debbie Haski-Leventhal. 'The Purpose-Driven University.' Transforming Lives and Creating Impact through Academic Social Responsibility, Emerald Group Publishing, 6/ 23/2020

The World Bank. 'The State of Social Safety Nets 2018.' World Bank Publications, 3/23/2018

Austin Pryor. 'Sound Mind Investing.' A Step-by-step Guide to Financial Stability & Growth, Sound Mind Investing, 1/1/2000

James K. Glassman. 'Safety Net.' The Strategy for De-Risking Your Investments in a Time of Turbulence, Crown, 2/22/2011

NARAYAN CHANGDER. 'COST MANAGEMENT.' THE AMAZING QUIZ BOOK, Changder Outline, 3/10/2024

Lynne A. Weikart. 'Budget Tools.' Financial Methods in the Public Sector, Greg G. Chen, CQ Press, 11/4/2014

Alfred B. Abraham. 'Analyze Your Records to Reduce Costs.' U.S. Small Business Administration, Office of Business Development, 1/1/1992

Brian T. Yates. 'Measuring and Improving Cost, Cost-effectiveness, and Cost-benefit for Substance Abuse Treatment Programs.' A Manual, U.S. Department of Health and Human Services, National Institutes of Health, 1/1/1999

Gil-Garcia, J. Ramon. 'E-Government Success around the World: Cases, Empirical Studies, and Practical Recommendations.' Cases, Empirical Studies, and Practical Recommendations, IGI Global, 6/30/2013

Center for Professional Responsibility (American Bar Association). 'Model Rules of Professional Conduct.' American Bar Association. House of Delegates, American Bar Association, 1/1/2007

J. Ward. 'Strategic Planning for The Family Business.' Parallel Planning to Unify the Family and Business, R. Carlock, Springer, 1/29/2001

Mauricio A Rostagno. 'Natural Product Extraction.' Principles and Applications, Juliana M Prado, Royal Society of Chemistry, 7/20/2022

Pinnacle Test Prep. 'PHR Study Guide 2025-2026.' 3 Full-Length Practice Tests + Comprehensive HRCI Certification Exam Preparation with 540 Detailed Questions and Expert Strategies, Nikky'ann Group LLC, 3/7/2025

Karen Kang. 'BrandingPays.' The Five-Step System to Reinvent Your Personal Brand, Branding Pays Media, 9/19/2020

Richard Gracia. 'The RICH Method.' The Definitive Guide to Getting Money and Success. Reduce Your Expenses, Clear Your Debts, Learn to Save and Invest, and Reach Your Financial Freedom., Independently Published, 3/24/2021

National Academy of Engineering. 'Building America's Skilled Technical Workforce.' National Academies of Sciences, Engineering, and Medicine, National Academies Press, 5/4/2017

Organisation for Economic Co-operation and Development. 'Women and Financial Education.' Evidence, Policy Responses and Guidance, OECD Publishing, 1/1/2013

Peter Nagle. 'Global Waves of Debt.' Causes and Consequences, M. Ayhan Kose, World Bank Publications, 3/4/2021

Andrei Shleifer. 'A Crisis of Beliefs.' Investor Psychology and Financial Fragility, Nicola Gennaioli, Princeton University Press, 9/11/2018

Jl Collins. 'The Simple Path to Wealth.' Your Road Map to Financial Independence and a Rich, Free Life, CreateSpace Independent Publishing Platform, 8/16/2021

Rachel S. Siegel. 'Personal Finance.' Flatworld., 1/1/2021

United States. Financial Crisis Inquiry Commission. 'The Financial Crisis Inquiry Report, Authorized Edition.' Final Report of the National Commission on the Causes of the Financial and Economic Crisis in the United States, PublicAffairs, 1/27/2011

Alistair McCleery. 'An Introduction to Book History.' David Finkelstein, Routledge, 3/13/2006

www.ingramcontent.com/pod-product-compliance
Lightning Source LLC
LaVergne TN
LVHW052312200926
848481LV00002B/543
9798231092338